Unlocking Social Skills for Teens

Go from awkward to awesome as you overcome social anxiety with practical exercises to use in real life as you empower yourself and thrive socially

Kimberly Myrick

Table of Contents

Introduction

Did you know that over 40% of teens report feeling social anxiety at some point? That's almost half the classroom, the cafeteria, or the soccer field feeling just as nervous as you might right at this moment. But what if I told you that it doesn't always have to be this way?

In this book, I'm on a mission to transform you from a socially awkward introvert into a confident social butterfly. I want to give you the tools not only to survive but to thrive in parties, school, and all sorts of social gatherings.

This isn't your average guide. I've tailored every chapter, and every exercise to be all about you—your world, your challenges, your potential. We'll tackle everything from starting conversations to maintaining friendships, all through practical, real-life exercises that I promise won't feel like just another class assignment.

What sets this book apart? It's built on understanding and inclusivity. I know that flipping through pages of theoretical advice can be dull. Hence, I've designed interactive elements and reflection points that will engage you actively and make the learning personal.

Here's what you can expect: a clear roadmap starting with the basics of communication, advancing through handling conflicts, and finally mastering group dynamics. Each section builds on the previous one, helping you gradually enhance your social toolkit.

Remember, improvement in social skills doesn't happen overnight. It's like learning to play an instrument or a new sport—it takes practice and patience. This book is here to be your companion, guiding you through each step, and cheering for your every little victory.

So, are you ready to take the first step? Engage with each exercise, reflect on your interactions, and watch as you change how you connect with others.

Let's turn those awkward moments into opportunities. Together, we'll make sure that your journey from anxiety to assurance isn't just successful, but also awesome.

Laying the Foundations of Social Interaction

Ever walked into a room and felt like everyone suddenly turned into a secret code of nods, smiles, and eyebrow raises that you just couldn't crack? Or maybe you've found yourself laughing along to a joke that you didn't quite catch but everyone else found hilarious. Welcome to the complex world of social cues—a land where a wink can mean a world of difference, and where the tone of "Hey" can either start a friendship or forecast a frosty feud.

Navigating this maze can seem daunting, especially if you're someone who feels a bit more comfortable at the edges of a party, clinging to your phone like a lifeline. But here's the good news: mastering the language of social cues isn't just for the "naturals" or those seemingly born with a charisma chip. This chapter is all about breaking down those invisible barriers, one gesture and expression at a time, transforming you into a fluent speaker of social cues. With a bit of practice and a dash of patience, you'll start to see that these mysterious signals are not just random, but are the keys to unlocking smoother and more meaningful interactions.

Understanding Social Cues: The Basics

Imagine you're watching your favorite TV show, but with the sound turned off. You might think you'd miss out on a lot, right? But if you pay close attention, you can still tell when characters are angry, happy, surprised, or sad just by watching their faces and body movements. That's the power of non-verbal communication, or what we call 'social cues.'

Social cues include facial expressions, tone of voice, and body language. These cues are critical because they help us understand how others are feeling and how they're responding to us without them needing to spell it out. For instance, if you crack a joke and the other person smiles with a slight eye roll, it's a cue that your joke was perhaps amusing but also a bit cheesy. Recognizing these cues is essential because it helps you navigate conversations and relationships more effectively.

But here's a kicker: social cues can change depending on where you are. The thumbs-up gesture might mean something positive in many parts of the world, but in the Middle East, it's offensive. Similarly, a casual chat with a friend can be full of slang and interruptions, but that same conversational style can seem rude in a more formal setting like a classroom discussion or job interview. Understanding the context is crucial to interpreting social cues correctly.

So, what happens when you misinterpret a cue? It's like using the wrong key in a lock—things won't open up as they should. Maybe you mistook someone's nervous laughter as them being amused, or their silence as agreement when they were actually uncomfortable. When you sense a misstep, don't panic. Use strategies like asking clarifying questions to make sure you're on the same page. For example, if you're not sure how someone felt about a comment, you could say, "I noticed you were pretty quiet after what I said about the movie. What did you think about it?" Observing how others react to the same situation can also provide clues about what's really going on.

One fun way to sharpen your skills at reading social cues is to watch a muted TV show or movie and try to interpret the characters' emotions and intentions just from their actions and expressions. You can even make a game out of it with friends or family members to see who guesses the context of the scene correctly. This exercise not only makes you more attuned to subtle non-verbal signals but also shows you how much communication happens without words.

As you become more observant of these social cues, you'll find yourself becoming more adept at navigating social waters. Whether it's catching the subtle sarcasm in a friend's voice or knowing when to change the topic during an awkward dinner conversation, mastering this unspoken language opens up a new dimension of connection with those around you. And before you know it what once felt like decoding hieroglyphics will start to feel like reading your favorite book—familiar, comfortable, and enjoyable.

The Art of the Introduction: How to Approach and Greet

Ever noticed how a movie character can walk into a room and instantly own it? They don't always have the loudest voices or the flashiest outfits, but somehow, everyone seems drawn to them. Well, that's the magic of mastering the art of introduction. Your first impression is like the cover of a book—it sets the stage for what's to come. This doesn't mean you need to perform dramatic entrances or wear neon signs. Sometimes, all it takes is a confident posture, a warm smile, and that spark of eye contact to say, "Hey, I'm glad to be here!"

The secret sauce? Confidence. And before you say, "But I'm not confident," hear me out. Confidence isn't something you're born with—it's something you can create. Start simple: stand straight, shoulders back, head high. It's not just about looking confident but feeling it too. When you meet someone, offer a smile. It's the universal signal that says, "I'm friendly and approachable." Then, lock eyes—not in a creepy, soul-staring contest, but in a gentle, I-see-you kind of way. It's about acknowledging their presence and showing you're genuinely interested in them.

Now, let's talk greetings. They can vary from handshakes to high-fives to even a nod, depending on whom you're meeting and where. In a formal setting like an internship interview, a firm handshake can show professionalism. At a casual meet-up with peers, maybe a fist bump or a wave works better. It's all about reading the room. For instance, if you're at a family gathering and your grandma is there, you wouldn't go for a high-five, right? A warm, respectful nod or a gentle hug suits you better. The key is to match the energy and expectations of the setting without losing your authenticity.

Imagine you're practicing these greetings with a friend. Role-playing various scenarios can boost your confidence significantly. Try different greetings, switch roles, and even give feedback to each other. It's like a rehearsal before the actual show, and it helps iron out any awkwardness. Think of it as a safe space to experiment with what type of greeting feels most natural and effective for you.

But what if nerves get in the way? It's normal to feel a flutter of butterflies in your stomach before meeting someone new. To manage this, breathe. Not the short, panicked breaths, but deep, calming ones. Breathe in slowly through your nose, hold it for a few seconds, and then exhale through your mouth. Repeat a few times. This not only calms your nerves but also centers your mind. Combine this with positive self-talk. Tell yourself, "I've got this," or "I'm really good at meeting new people." These little mantras can be incredibly soothing and empowering.

As you step into new social arenas, armed with a confident posture, a genuine smile, and the right greeting, you'll notice a shift not just in how others respond to you, but also in how you perceive yourself. It's about setting the tone for the interaction and, ultimately, the relationship. Whether it's making a new friend, acing a job interview, or simply getting to know a classmate better, the way you introduce yourself can open doors to more meaningful connections. And remember, each person you meet is a new chapter of experiences and opportunities—start it well.

Simple Conversation Starters: What to Say After "Hello"

So, you've mastered the smile, nailed the eye contact, and even got the handshake down to a T. But what comes next? Often, the hardest part of any conversation is just figuring out how to kick things off. Think of it like the first line of your favorite song—once you get past that, the rest comes with the rhythm. Whether you're in the halls at school, hanging out at a sports event, or at a party, having a few go-to conversation starters up your sleeve is like having the best snack at a party; it makes everyone want to join in.

Let's start with open-ended questions. These are the golden tickets to keeping a conversation flowing. They're the kind that requires more than just a yes or no answer. For instance, instead of asking someone, "Did you like the movie?" you could ask, "What did you think about the movie?" This slight tweak invites a more detailed response and shows that you're interested in their opinion, not just filling the silence. Another great one is, "What's your favorite memory from this summer?" It's personal, sparks nostalgia, and it's a great springboard into a deeper chat.

Now, depending on where you are, your conversation starter might change a bit. If you're at school, maybe ask about a class you both share: "Did you get what Mr. Smith was saying in history class today?" It's relevant and easy to relate to. At a sports event, tap into the excitement: "Which team are you cheering for?" Instant camaraderie! And at a party, try something fun like, "What's your favorite song on the playlist so far?" or even, "Have you checked out the photo booth? It's pretty fun." Each of these openers is tailored to fit the setting, making your approach feel natural and effortless.

Finding common ground can make this even easier. Start by observing your surroundings. Maybe you're both looking at the same piece of art at a gallery, or perhaps you've both grabbed the same bizarre-flavored soda at a barbecue. Use that as you're in. "Have you tried this drink before? I can't decide if I love it or hate it!" It's a simple line, but it breaks the ice and, just like that, you're having a conversation.

Balanced conversation is key. It's like a game of catch—if you don't throw the ball back, the game stops. Make sure you're not just firing off questions, but also sharing bits about yourself. If you ask someone about their favorite book, share yours too. It keeps the exchange mutual and engaging, showing that you're not conducting an interview but building a connection.

Handling silence can be tricky, but it doesn't have to be awkward. If you find yourself stuck, make a comment about something around you. Maybe there's a new song playing, or perhaps you can see something interesting happening nearby. "This new song is fire, don't you think?" or "Did you catch that amazing TikTok dance move?" It keeps things light and shifts the focus away from the silence.

What if you stumble? Maybe you forgot what you were going to say, or perhaps your mind just blanked. It happens to the best of us. Keep your cool, smile, and if you need to, use a filler like, "Sorry, I just lost my train of thought. What were we talking about?" It shows you're human and keeps the vibe friendly.

Lastly, never underestimate the power of a compliment. "I love your shoes! Where did you get them?" It's simple but effective. Everyone likes to feel good about their choices, whether it's their fashion or their fantastic taste in books. Just make sure your compliments are genuine and not overdone. It's about making the other person feel seen and appreciated, not overwhelmed.

To get you started, here are a couple of dialogue practices:

- At a school event: "This game is wild! Which part are you looking forward to the most?"
- At a party: "The music here is amazing! Which song has been your favorite so far?"

These starters are not just phrases, but bridges to learning more about others and letting them learn about you. It's about throwing the conversational ball and making sure it keeps going back and forth until you've both had a fun game. So next time you're standing there after saying hello, remember, you've got plenty to talk about.

Reading Body Language: Beyond Words

Have you ever noticed that sometimes what people say doesn't quite match up with how they say it? It's like when your friend says, "I'm fine," but their slumped shoulders and sad puppy eyes scream otherwise. Welcome to the complex world of body language, where the silent messages often shout the loudest. Mastering this silent language can give you a superpower-like ability to understand what people are really feeling, often before they've even fully processed it themselves. It's like being a social detective, decoding clues that are hidden in plain sight.

Body language includes all the non-verbal signals we use in communication: posture, gestures, facial expressions, and even the distance we keep from others. These cues can often tell you more about someone's true feelings than their words. For example, crossed arms might mean someone is feeling defensive or closed off, but they can also mean the person is just cold. That's why it's crucial not only to recognize these signals, but also to interpret them in context. A person who is crossing their arms while standing alone at a chilly bus stop is likely just trying to stay warm, not keeping the world at bay.

Other common body language signs include eye contact, or lack thereof. Consistent eye contact can signal confidence and honesty, whereas someone who frequently looks away might be nervous or hiding something. But again, context matters—a shy person might avoid eye contact because they're feeling overwhelmed, not because they're untrustworthy. Similarly, a genuine smile that reaches the eyes can indicate genuine happiness or approval, while a tight, lip-only smile might be masking discomfort or disapproval.

To get better at reading these silent signals, start observing people in real-life situations. It could be at your school cafeteria, during family gatherings, or while hanging out with friends. Pay attention to how people's body language changes depending on who they're talking to or what they're talking about. Notice how a teacher's posture might become more formal when the principal walks into the room, or how your sibling's face might light up when talking about their favorite video game. These observations can help you become more adept at picking up on and responding to the non-verbal cues that are all around you.

Practicing this kind of silent observation can dramatically improve your ability to communicate and connect with others. It helps you to respond more appropriately to friends and family, picking up on subtleties that might otherwise be missed. For instance, if you notice a friend's posture close off during a conversation, you might choose to steer the topic away from what's bothering them or ask if they're okay, showing that you respect and care about their feelings.

Remember, while body language can provide significant insights, it's not an exact science. People are complex, and various factors, including cultural differences, personal habits, and current mood, can influence how someone expresses themselves non-verbally. Always use your observations as a guide rather than a definitive answer, and consider the whole situation before jumping to conclusions.

By becoming fluent in the language of gestures and postures, you not only improve your ability to communicate with others but also open up a new dimension of understanding in your social interactions. This skill allows you to connect on a deeper level, build better relationships, and navigate social settings with greater ease and confidence. As you practice, you'll find yourself becoming more attuned to the unspoken dialogue happening all around you, enriching your interactions and helping you to become more empathetic and responsive to those in your social circle.

Listening Skills: Show That You Care

Have you ever caught yourself nodding along to a friend's long story while your mind is a million miles away, perhaps plotting your epic weekend or just daydreaming about lunch? We've all been there, but truly listening—like, genuinely absorbing what someone is saying—is both a rare and superpower skill in today's distraction-filled world. It's about more than just hearing words; it's about understanding, engaging, and responding in a way that makes the person talking truly feel seen and heard. This is where the magic of active listening comes into play.

Active listening is all about being fully present in a conversation. It involves giving your full attention to the speaker, showing them you're engaged with nods or appropriate facial expressions, and resisting the urge to interrupt their flow. This might sound simple, but with smartphones buzzing and a million other thoughts racing through our brains, giving someone your undivided attention can be quite a challenge. Yet, mastering this can transform your conversations from monologues into meaningful exchanges. It makes the speaker feel valued and shows you genuinely care about what they have to say, not just waiting for your turn to speak.

Distractions are the biggest thieves of effective communication. They sneak into conversations, often uninvited, through buzzing notifications or our own wandering thoughts. Minimizing these distractions is crucial for active listening. Start by putting away your phone or any other gadget that might draw your attention away from the conversation. If you're chatting in a noisy place, suggest moving somewhere quieter. Tell yourself that for these few moments, the person in front of you is the most important part of your world. This level of focus enhances the quality of your interactions and deepens your relationships.

Reflective listening is another key part of active listening. It involves paraphrasing or summarizing what the other person has said, not to parrot them, but to show that you're processing and understanding their message. It's like saying, "I see you, I hear you, and I get where you're coming from." For instance, if a friend tells you about a tough day at school, responding with, "It sounds like you had a really challenging day, especially with that test," can validate their feelings and encourage them to share more. It shows you're listening and empathizing with their situation.

Encouragement is also a crucial ingredient in active listening. Sometimes, all someone needs is a little nudge to keep sharing their thoughts or feelings. Simple phrases like, "What happened next?" or "How did that make you feel?" can do wonders. These cues can help the speaker open up more and delve deeper into their story. They signal that you're interested and invested in the conversation, making the speaker feel comfortable and appreciated.

Balancing listening with speaking is the final piece of the puzzle. Dominating conversations can be easy if you're excited or passionate about a topic, but remember, dialogue is a two-way street. Ensure you're not just waiting for your turn to talk, but are genuinely engaging with what's being said. This balance is crucial for healthy, reciprocal communication, where both parties feel equally heard and valued.

To hone your listening skills, try this exercise: next time you're catching up with a friend, challenge yourself to recall specific details about their story later. Were they excited about a new opportunity? Anxious about an upcoming event? After the conversation, see how much you can remember without checking texts or notes. This improves your attention and recall and makes your friend feel truly listened to and important.

By embracing these practices, you transform mere exchanges into meaningful conversations. Active listening makes others feel respected and valued and enriches your understanding of those around you, fostering deeper connections and making you a better friend, sibling, and classmate. So the next time someone is speaking to you, remember, it's not just about hearing them, it's about listening.

Expressing Your Thoughts Clearly and Confidently

Ever found yourself in a situation where you know exactly what you want to say, but the words that come out sound like they've been tossed into a blender? It's like, one minute you're confident, and the next, you're watching your words tumble out in a jumble that even confuses you. We've all been there, and let's be honest, it can be pretty frustrating. That's exactly why learning to express your thoughts clearly and confidently is a game-changer. It's not just about making a good impression; it's about being understood. This skill is crucial, whether you're giving a class presentation, explaining a point in a debate, or just chatting with friends.

First things first: structuring your thoughts. Imagine your thoughts as a library. If everything's just thrown in randomly, finding the book you need becomes a nightmare. But if it's organized—maybe alphabetically, by genre, or by author—suddenly everything is much easier to handle. The same goes for your thoughts. Before you speak, take a moment to sort through your ideas. Decide which point you want to make first, what details are important, and what can be left out. This mental organization will help you speak more fluidly, avoiding those awkward 'um's and 'uh's that sneak in when we're trying to think on the fly.

Now, let's talk about the words you choose. It's like selecting the right tool for the job. You wouldn't use a sledgehammer to crack a nut, right? Similarly, using overly complex vocabulary in everyday conversations can make your listeners more puzzled than impressed. Keep your language simple and direct to ensure clarity. But here's the twist: adapting your word choice depending on your audience and setting is key. Slang and casual language are great with friends but won't do you any favors in a school presentation or a job interview. Tailoring your language to your audience shows that you respect them and their context, which significantly boosts the effectiveness of your communication.

Voice modulation is your secret weapon here. It's not just about what you say; it's how you say it. Your tone, volume, and speed can completely change the message's impact. Imagine you're telling a story about something exciting— if you speak in a monotone voice, slowly and quietly, your listeners will be snoozing before you get to the good part. On the flip side, if you're discussing a serious topic, speaking too fast or too loudly might come off as aggressive. Practice adjusting these aspects of your speech to convey your emotions and intentions more accurately. It makes your communication dynamic and keeps your listeners engaged.

One of the best ways to put all these skills to the test is by getting involved in activities that require formal speaking, like debates or presentations. These platforms challenge you to think critically, organize your thoughts swiftly, and express them coherently. They also push you out of your comfort zone, which is where growth really happens. In a debate, for instance, you learn to formulate your thoughts under pressure, respond to counter arguments, and adjust your speaking style to persuade an audience. Each debate is a new opportunity to refine your structuring and delivery skills, not to mention a great way to build up your confidence.

Similarly, presentations offer a structured way to practice speaking clearly and effectively. They force you to plan your content, anticipate questions, and engage with your audience. It's not just about reading off slides; it's about making your message resonate. To excel, you need to bring in everything from structuring your talk to choosing the right words and modulating your voice to suit the setting and audience. Plus, the more presentations you do, the more naturally these skills will come to you.

So, whether it's stepping up for the debate team, leading a project presentation, or even teaching a class, take every chance to practice. Each time you speak in front of an audience, you're not just sharing what you know; you're also fine-tuning your ability to express yourself clearly and confidently. And who knows? With enough practice, you might just find yourself becoming the person who can think on their feet and speak from them impressively.

The Role of Empathy in Everyday Interactions

Empathy—sounds a bit like a buzzword that gets thrown around a lot, right? Like "synergy" in a business meeting or "metabolism" in a diet plan. But strip away the buzz, and what you're left with is a genuinely transformative skill, especially when it comes to building and nurturing relationships. So, what exactly is empathy? It's the ability to step into someone else's shoes, to understand and feel what they're going through from their perspective. It's different from sympathy, which is feeling pity or sorrow for someone else's misfortune. Empathy goes deeper—it's about connection, not just consolation.

Developing empathetic listening skills is like upgrading your communication software to the latest version—it enhances every interaction. It means really listening, not just waiting for your turn to speak. When someone shares something with you, try to grasp not only the words but the emotions behind them. Reflect on what's being said and offer responses that show you're engaged and understand. For example, if a friend is upset about not making the team, instead of saying something generic like "That's tough," you could say, "It sounds like you're really passionate about this sport. It must be really disappointing to not have the chance to show that right now." This kind of response shows that you're not just hearing them, but also feeling with them.

Empathy also plays a crucial role in resolving conflicts. Let's face it, disagreements are part of life, whether it's with siblings, friends, or classmates. But here's where empathy can be your secret peace-making weapon. By trying to see the other person's point of view, even if you don't agree with it, you can often find a path to understanding. It helps de-escalate tension because when people feel understood, they're more likely to be open to compromise. So, the next time you find yourself in a heated debate over who should have cleaned up or whose turn it is on the gaming console, take a moment. Try to understand where the other person is coming from. Maybe your sibling had a rough day and forgot about the chores, or perhaps your friend felt excluded the last time you played. Understanding these feelings can help smooth things over without turning into a full-blown battle.

Practicing empathy can start with simple exercises that you can try in your daily life. One effective method is to imagine how someone else is feeling. Next time you're watching a movie or reading a book, pause and think about the characters. What are they feeling at this moment? Why? You can do this with real people too. If you see someone looking upset or stressed, try to imagine what might be going on in their life. This doesn't mean you should make assumptions and gossip—it's about privately developing a deeper understanding of the emotions of others.

Another great exercise is sharing diverse life experiences with friends or family. Next time you're hanging out, share stories from your life and ask others to share theirs. Focus on how those experiences made you feel, not just the events themselves. This can help build a bridge of understanding and tolerance among your group because when you know someone's backstory, their actions and reactions start to make more sense. And who knows? This might just open the door to new insights about your own feelings and reactions.

Incorporating these practices into your daily life can significantly enhance your ability to connect with others. Whether it's resolving conflicts, deepening friendships, or just understanding your family better, empathy is a tool that can transform your interactions in a powerful way. So next time you find yourself in a tricky social situation, remember that empathy is your go-to strategy for navigating the complex world of human emotions and relationships.

How to Gracefully Change Uncomfortable Topics

Imagine you're knee-deep in a chat that's suddenly taken a turn into Awkwardville. Maybe your friend started ranting about politics when you just wanted to talk about the latest movie, or perhaps a group discussion is veering dangerously close to that one embarrassing story you'd rather forget. Yikes, right? But fear not! Steering a conversation away from touchy subjects without causing a scene or hurting feelings is a skill, and like any good skill, it comes with a few handy techniques up its sleeve.

First up, let's talk about recognizing discomfort. It's like being a social detective; you need to pick up on the subtle clues that scream, "This topic is as welcome as a rainstorm at a picnic." These signs could be as clear as someone outright saying, "Let's not talk about this," or as subtle as averted eyes, fidgeting, or even a shift in body language. Maybe your friend starts wrapping their arms tightly around themselves—a classic self-soothing move—or another suddenly finds the pattern on the tablecloth fascinating. These are your cues that it's time for a topic change, pronto.

Now, how do you change the topic without making it super obvious or making someone feel dismissed? This is where the art of the smooth transition comes in. It's like being a conversational magician; you redirect attention without anyone realizing you've done it. One way to do this is by bridging with related topics. For instance, if a debate about a school policy is getting heated, you might say, "Speaking of school, did anyone see the new mural they painted in the cafeteria? It's pretty amazing!" It shifts the focus but keeps the conversation flowing in a related, safer direction.

Humor is another incredible tool in your conversation toolkit. A well-timed joke or light-hearted comment can relieve tension and smoothly guide the dialogue towards happier territories. Let's say your group is arguing about a recent sports game that's starting to get a bit too passionate. You could chime in with something like, "Well, no matter who wins, I think we can all agree that my fantasy team is the real tragedy here." It's gentle, it's funny, and it offers a new, less contentious topic on a silver platter.

But here's where you need to tread carefully: tactfulness. This is critical because the last thing you want is to make someone feel like their thoughts or feelings are being dismissed or belittled. It's about acknowledging the current topic and why you're moving on, without making anyone feel bad about it. For example, if a conversation about a sensitive news event is causing discomfort, you could say, "I think we all have strong feelings about this, and it's really important. Maybe we could find a way to help or get involved instead of just feeling stuck in this discussion?" It shows you care about the issue and the people you're talking with, but it also redirects the energy towards something productive.

Practicing these techniques can make you a master of managing social dynamics, ensuring conversations remain enjoyable and comfortable for everyone involved. Next time you find yourself in the middle of a discussion that's turning sour, remember these strategies. With a little practice, you'll be switching topics so smoothly that even you won't realize you've done it until everyone's laughing and the storm has passed. So keep these tips in your back pocket, and ready yourself to tackle any conversational curve balls with grace and wit.

Mastering the Art of Small Talk in Different Settings

Let's be real: small talk can sometimes feel like trying to find your way through a corn maze—confusing, circular, and you're just hoping you bump into something interesting along the way. But here's a secret: mastering small talk is like having a Swiss Army knife in your social toolkit. It's not just chatter about the weather or what you had for lunch; it's your bridge to deeper conversations and lasting connections. Think of it as the appetizer before the main course—it sets the tone, whets the appetite, and gets things rolling. Whether you're navigating a nerve-wracking networking event, a casual hangout, or even a travel adventure, small talk is your first step towards building rapport and easing into those conversations that really matter.

So, how do you turn small talk from awkward to awesome? It's all about context. The way you chat at a family barbecue is different from how you might strike up a conversation at a professional workshop. Each setting has its own vibe and unwritten rules about what's cool to discuss. For instance, at a job fair, you might start by talking about the latest trends in your industry or asking about someone's experiences with their current company. It's relevant and shows you're not just there for the free pens and notepads. On the other hand, if you're at a concert, you might comment on the band's latest album or ask how they discovered the music. It's casual, relaxed, and keeps the ball rolling.

Navigating what topics to touch on can sometimes feel like tiptoeing through a minefield. There are the go-tos like hobbies, books, movies, or the event itself—safe ground for any conversation. Then there are the no-go zones like politics, personal finances, or overly personal questions that might make someone uncomfortable. Stick to topics that invite openness and are likely to generate positive vibes. Remember, the goal is to connect, not to debate or pry.

Improving your small talk game doesn't require a miracle—it just takes practice. Start small: chat with the barista when you grab your morning coffee, or make conversation with a classmate you haven't talked too much. Each little interaction builds your confidence and hones your skills. It's like leveling up in a video game, where each small talk scenario adds points to your charisma score. And don't forget to listen as much as you talk. Small talk is a two-way street; it's about exchange and flow. By showing genuine interest in the responses you get, you learn more about others and discover shared interests that can turn small talk into big connections.

Small talk might not save the world, but it can certainly open doors to new friendships, opportunities, and experiences. It's the oil that greases the wheels of social interaction, making it smoother and more enjoyable. So next time you find yourself in a situation where small talk is the ticket in, embrace it. Who knows? That chat about the weather might just lead to a storm of exciting new possibilities. So dive in, chat away, and watch as your world expands one conversation at a time.

Exiting Conversations Tactfully Without Offending Others

Knowing when and how to end a conversation gracefully is like mastering the art of leaving a party at just the right time —not too early that you miss out, and not too late that you overstay your welcome. It's a subtle skill that combines timing, tact, and a touch of foresight. Sometimes, recognizing when a chat has reached its natural conclusion can save both you and the other person from those dragging moments that feel like stretching a rubber band till it snaps— uncomfortable and possibly a little painful.

So, how do you spot the right moment to wrap things up? It's all about picking up on the cues. Maybe the conversation has covered all the bases, and you find yourselves rehashing topics already discussed. Or perhaps, despite the best efforts, there are more awkward silences than actual talking, and each pause grows longer than the last. These are your signals that it's time to bring things to a close. Another tell-tale sign is the body language—if the person you're chatting with starts glancing around the room, checking their phone, or even subtly edging towards the door, these are pretty clear indicators that the conversation has run its course.

Now, onto the art of exiting a conversation without making it awkward or offending anyone. The key here is to be as polite and positive as possible. Start with a kind word or a compliment about the interaction. Something like, "I really enjoyed our chat!" or "It was great catching up with you!" sets a positive tone. Then, lead into your exit with a polite excuse. You could say, "I promised to help a friend with something, so I'd better go find them," or "I need to head out soon, but let's catch up again later!" These kinds of phrases signal that you're leaving for a reason, not because you're bored or uninterested.

Another smooth strategy is proposing a future interaction. This shows that you value the relationship and are interested in continuing the conversation at another time. Try, "Let's talk more about this over coffee sometime!" or "I'd love to hear more about your trip—can we text about it later?" This gives you a natural exit and opens the door for future conversations, departure feels less like a goodbye and more like a 'see you later.'

Follow-up etiquette is often overlooked but just as important. Sending a quick message after your chat can make all the difference. A simple text saying, "Hey, I really enjoyed our conversation today! Let's definitely plan that coffee catch-up soon," reinforces the positive interaction and shows that you meant what you said about staying in touch. It keeps the connection alive, making your next meeting feel more like picking up where you left off, rather than starting from scratch.

Mastering these nuances of conversation can turn you into a communication wizard—someone who knows not only how to keep a conversation going but also how to end one smoothly and maintain relationships long after. It's about being mindful, considerate, and proactive in your social interactions, ensuring that every conversation you have builds bridges rather than burning them. So next time you find yourself ready to exit a chat, remember these tips, and you'll be able to leave on a high note, keeping both your social grace and your connections intact.

Understanding and Managing Social Anxiety as an Introvert

Have you ever felt like attending a loud party feels akin to being a cat at a dog convention? If yes, you might just be an introvert navigating through a world that can't stop talking. But fear not, being an introvert isn't a hurdle to overcome—it's a unique perspective to embrace, especially when it comes to managing social anxiety. This chapter is dedicated to digging deep into what it means to be an introvert, how it impacts your life, and how you can wield your introverted qualities like a master swordsman in a social duel.

Understanding Introverts: What it is and isn't

The term 'introvert' gets tossed around a lot, often wrapped in many misconceptions. But let's set the record straight. Clinically speaking, introversion is a personality trait characterized by a preference for quiet, minimally stimulating environments. Introverts are not necessarily shy (which is a fear of social judgment), but they do recharge their energy by spending time alone, contrasting with extroverts, who gain energy from being around other people.

Now, introverts come in all shapes and flavors. Some might be the contemplative, book-loving types, while others can handle social gatherings but feel drained afterward. Common traits among introverts include a penchant for deep thinking and a greater need for personal space. This introspective nature often makes introverts great listeners and detail-oriented individuals—a superpower not to be underestimated!

In terms of daily life, being an introvert can color your experiences in several ways. In school, introverted teens might find group projects or speaking up in class more draining than their extroverted peers would. Social events might require a mental pep talk (or three), and the idea of small talk could be mildly terrifying. But it's crucial to remember that these reactions are perfectly normal and manageable.

One of the most persistent myths is that introverts are just shy or antisocial. Not true! Being an introvert doesn't automatically mean you're shy; it simply means you enjoy solitude and might feel overwhelmed by excessive socializing or overly stimulating environments. Another common misconception is that introversion is a flaw that needs to be fixed. Nope, it's actually a built-in filter system allowing you to dive deep into your thoughts and feelings—pretty neat, right?

Take a moment to reflect on how being an introvert affects your daily activities. Think about the last time you felt drained from an interaction. What could have been done differently? Reflecting on these instances can help you better manage similar situations in the future.

By understanding and embracing your introverted nature, you can navigate social landscapes more effectively and use your intrinsic qualities to your advantage. Remember, every personality trait, including introversion, comes with its own set of superpowers. It's all about knowing how to use them. So, the next time you find yourself dreading that family gathering or school event, remind yourself that your introverted traits are not just quirks—they're your strengths.

Understanding Yourself

Exploring your own level of introversion isn't just about slapping a label on yourself and calling it a day. It's about diving into the nitty-gritty of what makes you tick in social situations. Think of it as becoming your own social scientist, where every interaction gives you data about what environments light you up and which ones make you want to run for the hills. This kind of self-assessment is crucial because it helps you navigate your social world more effectively, making sure you're playing to your strengths rather than constantly battling against your natural tendencies.

Start by paying attention to how you feel during and after different types of social interactions. Do large parties leave you feeling drained or invigorated? When you have a deep conversation with a friend, how does that feel compared to small talk at a networking event? These feelings are your clues. You might find that certain types of interactions are genuinely enjoyable, while others feel like you're trying to walk through mud. It's all about spotting patterns. Maybe you're okay with big gatherings as long as you have a clear role to play, like being the photographer at a party, which can give you a sense of purpose and a way to engage that doesn't feel overwhelming.

Embracing your introverted nature is like embracing a superpower. It's about seeing your preference for less stimulating environments not as a limitation but as a unique strength. For instance, introverts often have the superpower of being able to dive deep into subjects, making them great at things like writing, art, coding, or any field that requires a lot of focus and depth. They're also often good at building close, meaningful relationships—a few good friends rather than a whole squad of acquaintances. This isn't a flaw; it's a feature!

To truly embrace your introversion, start by redefining what success in social situations looks like for you. It doesn't have to mean being the life of the party or the last one to leave. Maybe it means having a couple of meaningful conversations or just enjoying observing the dynamics around you. Set your own benchmarks based on what feels fulfilling to you, not on some extrovert's idea of a good time. And remember, there's great strength in being someone who can sit comfortably with their thoughts, who can listen deeply to a friend, or who brings a thoughtful perspective to a conversation. These are traits that the world needs, especially in an age where everything seems to move at breakneck speed.

Create a simple chart to log different social settings you find yourself in each week. For each setting, write down how energized or drained you felt afterward, and any particular aspects that contributed to those feelings. This visual tracking can help you see patterns over time, making it easier to make informed decisions about which engagements you choose to dive into.

By understanding and embracing your introversion, you're not setting up barriers; you're building bridges—bridges that connect you to experiences and people in ways that feel right for you. This self-knowledge allows you to navigate your social world with more confidence and less burnout, showing that sometimes, the quietest person in the room can often have the richest inner world. So, as you move forward, carry with you the knowledge that your introverted traits aren't just okay; they're your hidden superpowers in a world that can't stop talking.

Strategies to Manage Social Anxiety as an Introvert

Let's face it, even thinking about attending a big event can sometimes feel like you're gearing up for a trek across a glacier—daunting and a little bit chilly in the excitement department. But don't sweat it! One of the coolest strategies in the introvert's toolkit is simply planning ahead. Knowing what you're walking into can massively dial down the anxiety meter. It's like having a map in a video game; the more you know about the terrain, the better you can navigate it.

So, how do you get this magical map? Start simple: gather details about the event. Who's going to be there? What's the occasion? Is there a program or a schedule? Understanding the structure of the event can help you spot opportunities to engage in ways that feel comfortable to you. For example, if there will be a group activity or a quiet corner for chilling, you can plan to spend your energy there. It's like choosing your battlefield, and believe me, the right battleground can make all the difference.

Now, let's talk about the power of familiarity. If possible, visit the venue beforehand. Knowing the physical layout can ease your mind—no need to worry about getting lost or not knowing where the bathrooms are when you need a minute to yourself. If a pre-visit isn't possible, try looking up photos online or asking the host about the venue. Even a rough mental image can help reduce the unknowns and make the whole scenario less intimidating.

Another hot tip? Have an escape plan. No, not the dramatic kind involving smoke bombs and rappelling out the nearest window, but a simple, thought-out plan for stepping away if things get overwhelming. Maybe it's a code word with a friend or a set time you'll allow yourself a breather. Just knowing you have an out can make a big difference in how secure you feel. And remember, it's totally okay to take breaks. Social stamina isn't a competition. It's about enjoying yourself and managing your energy in a way that feels right for you.

Here's a quick checklist for your next social event:

- Event Info Gathering: Date, time, location, attendees, schedule.
- Venue Recon: Layout familiarity—entrances, exits, rest areas.
- Plan Your Participation: Identify parts of the event you are likely to enjoy.
- Escape Plan: Decide on signs you need a break and how you'll take it.

Armed with this information and a solid plan, you're much more equipped to handle the social pressures that come your way. It turns a looming mountain into a series of small, manageable hills. And before you know it, you'll find yourself navigating social events with a newfound confidence, perhaps even surprising yourself with how adept you've become at handling what once felt like insurmountable challenges. So next time an invitation lands in your lap, instead of defaulting to panic mode, take a moment to strategize. With a little preparation, you might just find yourself looking forward to it.

Leveraging Technology

In the digital age, introverts can find a unique comfort in the realm of technology. It's like having a secret passageway that bypasses the bustling crowds and leads directly to a calm, controlled environment where social interactions don't demand an immediate physical presence. Let's dive into how you can use digital tools and online platforms to gently ease into social interactions, turning what might feel like a daunting process into a manageable and even enjoyable one.

Social media and other online platforms offer a buffer that the face-to-face immediacy of in-person interactions lacks. Think of it as a rehearsal space for your social skills. Here, you have the chance to craft your responses with care, free from the pressure of someone watching your every facial expression or hearing the uncertainty in your voice. For an introvert, this can mean the difference between a stressful interaction and a positive one. You get to control the pace, the space, and the intensity, making these digital interactions a less energy-draining part of your social life.

Platforms like Facebook, Instagram, or Twitter can be fantastic tools for initiating and maintaining connections. Start by engaging with content that interests you. Leave a comment on a post, share a story that resonates, or even send a direct message to someone you admire. These actions allow you to interact without the overhead of continuous engagement required in physical settings. Plus, the asynchronous nature of these platforms means you can respond when you feel ready, not rushed. It's about making socializing something you can manage on your own terms, allowing you to express your thoughts and personality in a way that feels authentic and comfortable.

Now, venturing into online communities might seem a bit like stepping into a party where you don't know anyone. But here's the twist—everyone's there because they share a common interest or passion. Sites like Reddit, Discord, or even specific Facebook groups can be gold mines for connecting with people who get excited about the same obscure band, vintage comic books, or niche hobby as you do. These platforms offer a sense of belonging and community that can be hard to replicate in your immediate physical surroundings, especially if your interests aren't shared by your peers.

When you join these online communities, start small. You might begin by reading discussions and seeing how others interact. As you grow more comfortable, start contributing to the conversations. Post a question, share an insight, or offer support to someone else. Each positive interaction builds your confidence, not just in navigating online spaces but in your social skills overall. Think of each little interaction as a step towards building a more confident social version of yourself, one click at a time.

The real magic of these digital interactions lies in their ability to highlight your unique talents and perspectives, offering opportunities for expression that you might not find in conventional social environments. You can show your witty side with a clever tweet, share your perspective in a blog post, or even showcase your artistic skills on Instagram. Each platform offers a different stage, a different audience, and a unique way for you to express yourself. And the best part? You can do it all from the comfort of your favorite chair, at your own pace, in your own space.

By embracing these digital tools, you're not hiding from the world; you're just choosing to interact with it on your terms. It's about using technology not as a crutch, but as a bridge that helps you connect with others in a way that respects your introverted nature while still allowing you to grow your social circle. So next time you log on, see it not just as scrolling through your feed but as stepping into your arena, where you can be both comfortably introverted and confidently social.

Set Realistic Goals

Setting goals might sound like something your coach shouts about on the field, but when it comes to managing social anxiety, it's less about scoring points and more about finding your comfort zone at your own pace. Think of setting social goals as creating a personalized roadmap that gently guides you through social situations without overwhelming pressure. It's like choosing a hiking trail that matches your current fitness level—you wouldn't start with Mount Everest, right? So, setting realistic, achievable goals for social interactions can definitely ease up the anxiety and make the whole 'socializing thing' feel more like a fun challenge than a dreaded chore.

Let's break it down: starting with setting realistic expectations. Say you're going to a party. Instead of setting an overwhelming goal like, 'I need to be the life of the party,' how about something more manageable? For instance, 'I'll try to have a good conversation with at least three people.' It's specific, measurable, and most importantly, achievable. This way, you're not setting yourself up for disappointment by aiming for something out of your comfort zone. Instead, you're creating a target that challenges you but doesn't push you too far too fast. It's about acknowledging where you are on your social skills journey and setting a marker just one step ahead, not ten.

Now, about taking small steps—this is where the magic happens. Imagine you're at the same party, and you've spotted someone you'd like to talk to. Instead of diving straight into deep philosophical discussions or personal questions, why not start small? A simple 'Hey, I like your shirt, where did you get it?' can open up the conversation without putting too much pressure on either of you. These small, low-risk interactions build up your confidence bit by bit, making it easier over time to handle more prolonged or deeper conversations. The more you engage, the more skilled you become, turning what once seemed like daunting challenges into manageable quests.

In this ongoing process, remember that every little step counts. Each conversation you start, each question you ask, and each time you choose to step out of your comfort zone, you're building your social stamina. It's not about being perfect; it's about being a little better than you were yesterday. So, give yourself the grace to grow at your own pace, celebrating the small victories along the way. These moments of triumph, no matter how minor they might seem, are the building blocks of your growing confidence. They're proof that you can do this, one realistic goal at a time.

Utilize Your Strengths

When you think about superpowers, your mind might instantly go to flying, invisibility, or super-strength. But what if I told you that as an introvert, you possess some pretty incredible powers too? Let's explore how these inherent qualities can enhance your social interactions and turn you into someone others lean on and respect.

Now, think about the last time you really listened to someone. Not just hearing their words while you mentally recount your day, but truly listening—catching the inflections in their voice, noting their body language, understanding the emotions behind their words. Introverts, like you, often naturally excel at this. You have this amazing gift because your energy is not scattered all over the place; it's focused. This makes you an excellent listener. People love being heard—it makes them feel valued and understood. So when you listen intently, you're not just gathering information, you're giving the speaker a gift: the gift of recognition and validation. This doesn't just apply to deep, soul-searching conversations; it's equally important in everyday chats. Whether it's a friend venting about a tough day or a classmate explaining a complex concept, your attentive listening can strengthen your connections, making others feel supported and appreciated.

But how do you leverage this in your daily interactions? Start by showing that you're engaged. Nod occasionally, make eye contact, and maybe throw in a verbal acknowledgement now and then, like "That sounds really challenging," or "I can see why you'd feel that way." These small actions can make a huge difference in how people perceive your attentiveness. Also, remember, good listening also involves patience—allow the conversation to unfold naturally without rushing to fill silences or jumping to provide solutions. Sometimes, people just need to talk things out to find their own answers.

Switching gears to your thoughtful nature—another introvert superpower. Your ability to reflect deeply on issues can bring new perspectives and ideas to any conversation. This thoughtfulness means you're likely to consider the implications of what's being said, which can lead to more meaningful and constructive discussions. You're not just thinking about what to say next; you're considering what's being said now. This can make you a great problem-solver, someone who brings new solutions and ideas to the table.

To make the most of this trait, don't be afraid to take your time before you respond in conversations. It's okay to say, "Let me think about that for a second." This not only gives you time to formulate your thoughts but also shows others that you're considering their words seriously, which can increase their respect for you. Additionally, when you do offer thoughts or solutions, frame them in a way that shows you've listened and reflected. For example, "Thinking about what you said, it looks like going with this plan might actually work because..." This not only showcases your reflective abilities but also cements your role as a thoughtful contributor in any social setting.

By embracing and utilizing your listening and reflective skills, you transform your introverted tendencies into tools for building stronger, more meaningful relationships. You prove that being quiet doesn't mean being passive—it means being a powerful presence that adds depth and value to interactions. So the next time you're in a social situation, remember these aren't just quirks of your personality; they're your superpowers. Use them wisely, and watch as your social world transforms, not into an exhausting battlefield, but into a stage where your strengths shine brightly, helping you connect with others in ways that are both fulfilling and impactful.

Practice Self-Care

After a bustling day of mingling and chatting, ever felt like your social battery didn't just run low—it completely fizzled out? Yup, that's a classic introvert hangover. Unlike our extrovert pals who gain energy from social interactions, we introverts spend our energy, and sometimes we spend a little too much without realizing it. Think of it like using a phone all day without bothering to check the battery level—eventually, it's going to power down. That's why understanding the need to recharge and knowing how to do it effectively is crucial for any introvert, especially when navigating the social labyrinth.

Recharging for introverts is not about avoiding social interactions or shying away from others; rather, it's a vital act of self-care to prevent your mental energy from depleting. Picture this: you've just spent a few hours at a friend's birthday party, chatting and laughing. While fun, it can be quite draining. This is where the art of recharging comes into play. It's about giving yourself permission to step back, to find a quiet space where the only expectation is to simply be. For some, this might mean curling up with a good book or binging a favorite show. For others, it might involve sketching, playing an instrument, or taking a long walk. The key is to engage in activities that refill your energy rather than demand more of it. It's not just about being alone—it's about being with yourself in a way that brings peace and restoration.

Mindfulness and relaxation techniques are another cornerstone of effective self-care. These aren't just trendy buzzwords; they are practical tools that can help you manage anxiety and maintain your mental health. Let's start with mindfulness. This practice involves being fully present in the moment, aware of where we are and what we're doing, without being overly reactive or overwhelmed by what's going on around us. It can be as simple as paying attention to your breathing, noticing the air moving in and out of your lungs, or feeling the sensations of your feet hitting the ground as you walk. This helps anchor you in the now, clearing the clutter of past interactions and future worries— a mental reset button if you will.

Relaxation techniques, on the other hand, are about consciously directing your body to transition from a state of tension to one of calm. Techniques such as deep breathing exercises, progressive muscle relaxation, or even guided imagery can be powerful allies in your self-care arsenal. For instance, try the 4-7-8 breathing method post-social events: breathe in deeply for 4 seconds, hold that breath for 7 seconds, and exhale slowly for 8 seconds. This technique is known for its ability to reduce anxiety and induce a state of calm, almost like giving your nervous system a soothing massage. Making these practices part of your daily routine, especially after intense social interactions, can significantly improve how you recover and how quickly you're ready to dive back into the bustling world outside your comfort zone.

Incorporating these self-care strategies into your life isn't just about feeling better in the moment; it's about building resilience over time. It's about creating a buffer that softens the impact of social exhaustion and protects your mental energy. By regularly practicing mindfulness and relaxation, you're not just recovering faster; you're fortifying yourself against the mental drain that can come from future interactions. This proactive approach to self-care ensures that you're not just surviving your social life, but thriving within it, fully equipped to handle the ebbs and flows of social energy demands. So next time you feel your social battery draining, remember these techniques. Consider these strategies your unique arsenal, a safeguard against feeling overwhelmed, guaranteeing that you can embrace social interactions in a way that respects your personal boundaries and health.

Seek Support

When you're feeling like social situations are more of a puzzle than a party, it's not just okay to seek support—it's actually a pretty smart move. Imagine you're trying to solve a really tough math problem. You could spend hours banging your head against the wall, or you could reach out to a buddy or a tutor. Suddenly, what seemed impossible starts to look a lot more manageable. The same goes for navigating the maze of social interactions. You don't have to figure it all out on your own. Talking to someone you trust can be like finding a guide in the social wilderness, someone who can offer you a map, some encouragement, and maybe even a few expert tips.

Reaching out can start with a conversation with a friend, a family member, or even a counselor. These chats can be your safe space, where you can express what feels overwhelming or confusing without the fear of judgment. It's like opening up a pressure valve—sometimes, just the act of talking things through can lighten your load and make everything seem a bit clearer. Plus, these people often come with their own experiences and insights, which means they might just have the advice you need. For example, maybe your older sibling has navigated similar struggles, or perhaps your counselor has some strategies up their sleeve that you haven't considered. These perspectives can be invaluable, giving you new tools to handle old problems.

But what if you're thinking, "I don't really have anyone like that"? Or what if you're just not comfortable sharing these things with people you know? That's where support groups come into play. These are spaces filled with people who are riding the same emotional roller coaster as you are. They understand the ups and downs because they're right there with you. Finding a support group might seem daunting, but it's actually easier than you might think. Start with a quick search online for groups in your area or online communities focused on social anxiety or introversion. Look into forums and social media groups where people share and discuss their experiences with social anxiety.

Joining a support group offers a double whammy of benefits. First, it's reassuring to see that you're not alone in your struggles. There's a whole tribe of people out there who get what you're going through because they're facing the same challenges. This can be incredibly comforting and a powerful antidote to the isolation that often comes with social anxiety. Secondly, these groups often share strategies and coping mechanisms. It's like crowd sourcing solutions to your social dilemmas. You might learn about techniques you've never considered before, or you might find new motivation to revisit strategies that you've tried in the past. Plus, as you get more comfortable, you might find that you have insights and advice to offer others, which can be a big boost to your confidence.

It's important to remember that seeking support is not a sign of weakness; it's a strategy for strength. Whether it's opening up to someone close or joining a group of like-minded individuals, taking this step can be a game-changer. It's about building a network of allies who can stand with you as you navigate the social world. With each conversation, each meeting, you're not just collecting advice and strategies; you're also building resilience and expanding your support system. This network can become a powerful tool, transforming the daunting journey of managing social anxiety into a more navigable path. So, take a deep breath and reach out. You might just find the support you need to turn your social challenges into opportunities for growth and connection.

Overcoming Social Anxiety

Have you ever been at a gathering, holding a plate of snacks, while trying to figure out the perfect spot to stand that makes you appear approachable yet keeps you at a comfortable distance from too much conversation? If that's a resounding "yes," then you, my friend, might be grappling with social anxiety. It's like having an awkward little gremlin on your shoulder that whispers doom into your ear right as you're about to strike up a conversation. But here's the kicker: you're not alone, and this gremlin isn't unbeatable. Let's take the power back from this unwelcome guest and learn how to navigate social waters with confidence, shall we?

Understanding Social Anxiety: What It Is and Isn't

First off, let's clear up what social anxiety is NOT. It's not just feeling a bit nervous before giving a presentation or worrying about a first date. Those butterflies are normal;

they're a part of life's rich tapestry of "oh-crap" moments. Social anxiety, on the other hand, is more persistent. It's like your brain's alarm system going haywire, telling you there's danger when all you're doing is ordering a pizza over the phone.

Clinically speaking, social anxiety is defined as the intense, persistent fear of being watched and judged by others. This fear can affect everyday activities, making things like talking to classmates, participating in sports, or even raising your hand in class feel overwhelming. It's not just shyness; it's a fear so intense it can buckle your knees.

Now, let's talk about symptoms. These can range from the classics like excessive sweating, trembling, and rapid heartbeat to less obvious signs like rigid body posture, mind going blank, or nausea. It's your body's way of saying, "I'm definitely not okay with this situation." Triggers can vary widely, but common ones include performing or being the center of attention, interacting with strangers, and, ironically, attending social events where the main agenda is to chill and have fun.

Social anxiety extends its reach beyond just hampering your social interactions; it can cast a shadow over your academic achievements and personal connections as well. It might make you avoid group projects or social gatherings, leading to a Hogwarts-sized castle of isolation. But before you hang your hat on the hermit's hook, let's bust some myths.

One of the biggest myths is that social anxiety is just a fancy term for being overly introverted. Not true. As we've discussed in the previous chapter, introversion is a personality trait where individuals prefer calm, minimally stimulating environments. Social anxiety, however, is a recognized anxiety disorder—it's not a preference or a personality quirk. Another myth? That you can just "snap out of it." If overcoming social anxiety were that simple, it wouldn't be such a common hurdle. It takes understanding, strategies, and sometimes professional help to manage it effectively.

Take a moment to reflect on how social anxiety might be showing up in your life. Which situations feel like they're setting off your internal alarm? Recognizing these can be a powerful first step in managing your anxiety.

By understanding what social anxiety really is—and what it isn't—you can begin to remove the stigma, open up conversations, and take the first steps toward managing it effectively. Remember, knowledge is power. The more you know about what you're dealing with, the better equipped you'll be to kick that gremlin off your shoulder and step into social situations with confidence. So, let's keep this momentum going as we explore more strategies to tackle social anxiety, ensuring it doesn't get the best of you. After all, every great warrior needs a solid battle plan, right? Let's craft yours.

Identifying Your Social Anxiety Triggers

Imagine you're about to step on stage. The crowd is buzzing, lights are dazzling, and just as you take your first step, your stomach flips. Sound familiar? That's your personal anxiety gremlin doing its thing, ringing the alarm bells for what it thinks is a full-blown crisis. But what if you could train yourself to recognize these alarms, understand them, and manage them better? That's what identifying your social anxiety triggers is all about. Think of it as becoming the boss of your own brain's panic button.

So, how do you start this process of becoming the boss? It begins with awareness. By pinpointing the specific situations, people, or expectations that trip your anxiety alarms, you gain the first piece of the puzzle in managing your reactions. For instance, does the thought of speaking in front of the class make your palms sweat? Or maybe it's the buzzing cafeteria that sends your heart into overdrive. Recognizing these triggers is like mapping out the minefield so you can navigate through it more safely.

One effective way to keep track of these triggers is by maintaining a self-observation log. Yes, it sounds a bit like homework, but this isn't about grades; it's about gaining insights into your own patterns. Each day, jot down moments when you felt anxious and what was happening at the time. Was it during a sudden group project announcement, or perhaps during lunch when you sat with a new group? Over time, you'll start to see patterns emerge, and like connecting the dots, these patterns will guide you to your major triggers.

Understanding your reactions, both physical and emotional, is also crucial. Physical signs of anxiety are often the first giveaway that your brain has hit the panic button. These can include an accelerated heartbeat, sweating, trembling, or even feeling dizzy. On the emotional side, you might notice feelings of dread, a blank mind, or an overwhelming urge to flee. Recognizing these signs early on gives you a chance to employ strategies to calm down before they escalate.

Now, let's talk about mastering mental preparation and squashing those negative thoughts. Negative self-talk can be like a soundtrack of doom playing in your head, and it's about time you changed the tune. Start with positive affirmations. These are positive statements about yourself that you repeat often to challenge and undermine harmful beliefs. Phrases like "I am capable of handling this situation," or "I am becoming better at managing social settings," can slowly help reshape your perceptions. Also, set realistic interaction goals before social situations. Instead of aiming to be the star of the show, maybe your goal is to have a meaningful conversation with just one or two people. Small, achievable goals can gradually build your confidence without overwhelming you. So take a deep breath, hold your head high and tell yourself "I've got this".

Don't underestimate the power of a second opinion. Sometimes, our own perceptions can be a bit skewed by anxiety. Talking to someone you trust about what you've observed can provide a new perspective. Maybe your teacher has noticed that you participate effectively when you're prepared with notes, or a friend might point out that you seem really engaged when discussing topics you love. This feedback can be incredibly valuable, providing external confirmation of your own observations and suggesting new areas for improvement.

By taking these steps—recognizing your triggers, logging your observations, understanding your reactions, preparing mentally, and seeking feedback—you're equipping yourself with the knowledge and tools to manage your social anxiety more effectively. It's about taking control of the situation, understanding your responses, and actively working towards change. So, grab that journal, start logging, chat with your confidants, and set yourself up for success. You're not just at the mercy of your anxiety; you have the power to understand it, manage it, and thrive despite it.

Breathing Techniques for Immediate Calm

Ever felt like your nerves were a soda can, all shaken up and ready to explode before a big presentation or during a party where you barely know anyone? Well, before you pop the top and fizz over, let's talk about a secret weapon you can use to keep your cool – breathing techniques. Yeah, it might sound a bit like something your yoga-obsessed aunt might suggest, with her incense and herbal teas, but trust me, it's backed by science and can be a total game-changer in managing your social anxiety.

First up, let's break down a simple yet powerful technique: deep breathing. It's like hitting the reset button on your body's stress response. Here's how you do it: Find a quiet place where you can sit comfortably, or even stand if you like – just make sure your posture is relaxed but upright. Now, breathe in slowly through your nose, counting to four in your head, feeling the air filling your lungs. Hold that breath for a second or two, then exhale through your mouth for another count of four. The key here is to focus on your breath, imagine it sweeping through your body, calming everything down like a gentle wave smoothing out the sand. Repeat this cycle four or five times, and you'll notice a sense of calm washing over you, proving that sometimes, the best solutions are literally a breath away.

Now, while deep breathing is awesome on its own, pairing it with visualization techniques can amplify the effects. Here's what you do: as you breathe in deeply, picture a scene in your mind that's calming. Maybe it's a quiet beach at sunset, the waves gently lapping at the shore, or a cozy cabin in the woods, the air crisp and fresh. As you exhale, imagine blowing out all the stress and tension, like dark smoke clearing away. To add another layer, visualize yourself succeeding in a social situation. See yourself chatting confidently at a party, or nailing your speech in class. This mental rehearsal primes your brain to act the part when the time comes because you've already seen yourself doing it in your mind's eye.

Progressive muscle relaxation takes this a step further by involving your body more directly. Start by tensing a group of muscles as you breathe in, say your fists or your toes, hold them tight for a moment, and then release all that tension as you breathe out. Move through different muscle groups – your legs, your stomach, your arms – tensing each one and then letting go. It's like giving your body a mini massage. By the time you've worked through your body, you'll find the physical symptoms of anxiety, like that knot in your stomach or that tightness in your chest, have lessened, making you feel more relaxed and grounded.

To make these techniques truly effective, especially when you're under pressure, practice is key. It's like training for a sport – the more you practice, the better you get, and the more naturally it comes to you when it counts. Try to set aside a few minutes each day to practice these breathing exercises. It doesn't have to be long – even just five minutes daily can make a significant difference. Make it a part of your routine, maybe each morning before you start your day, or in the evening as you wind down. Regular practice not only helps you get better at these techniques but also makes it easier to employ them automatically when anxiety starts to creep in.

So, whether you're about to step into a crowd or up to the podium, remember, your breath is a powerful tool. It's always with you, completely free, and doesn't require any special equipment. With these techniques in your back pocket, you'll be ready to face those social challenges with a sense of calm and confidence. Now, take a deep breath, and let's keep moving forward.

Preparing Mentally for Social Events

Imagine you're gearing up for the social Olympics, where the events range from casual hangouts to high-energy parties. The secret to not just surviving but thriving? It's all in the mental prep. Think of your mind as your personal coach, gearing you up to take on the social world with confidence and ease. The first step in this mental workout plan is setting realistic expectations. It's like aiming to score a personal best, rather than vying for a world record every time you step out. For instance, if mingling at parties feels like wrestling a gorilla, don't set yourself up with the goal of being the star entertainer. Instead, aim to have a few pleasant conversations. This approach shifts your focus from daunting to doable, reducing the pressure and dialing down the anxiety. Setting achievable goals keeps your spirits up and builds a ladder of small successes you can climb, one step at a time.

Now, let's jazz things up with some positive imagery. Picture this: before every major athlete performs, they visualize their success. You can do the same for social scenarios. Spend a few minutes picturing yourself nailing that interaction at the party or connecting well with a new classmate. Imagine the smiles, the laughter, and the easy exchanges. This isn't just fanciful thinking; it's a technique proven to boost your mental state and confidence. By visualizing positive outcomes, you're paving neural pathways that prime your brain to act out those successes in real life. It's like rehearsing a play before the curtain rises. When you've already seen yourself succeed in your mind's eye, doing it for real feels a lot less intimidating.

Cognitive rehearsal takes this a step further. This technique involves mentally walking through a challenging social situation step by step. Think about what you'll say, how you might respond to comments, and even plan some exit strategies for sticky scenarios. For example, if you're worried about running out of things to say, think about a few interesting topics in advance, like a new movie you enjoyed or a book you're reading. This preparation works like a safety net, giving you a sense of control and readiness. It's about scripting your own success story in your head before the event, making you feel prepared and reducing those pesky what-if anxieties.

Before you step into your next social event, having a pre-game relaxation ritual can help calm those jitters. Here's a simple checklist to chill out and get in the right headspace:

- Deep Breathing: Spend a few minutes doing some deep breathing exercises. Inhale slowly through your nose, hold for a few seconds, and exhale through your mouth. Repeat until you feel calmer.

- Listen to Music: Put on some tunes that lift your spirits or calm your nerves. Whether it's smooth jazz or your favorite pop songs, let the music set a positive tone.
- Stretch It Out: Do some light stretching to release tension in your body. Neck rolls, shoulder shrugs, or arm stretches can do wonders.
- Positive Affirmations: Give yourself a pep talk. Use positive affirmations like "I am calm and confident" or "I am open and ready to enjoy myself." Say them out loud or in your head to boost your morale.

Incorporating these techniques into your routine before social events can significantly lower your stress levels, making you feel more relaxed and prepared. It's like putting on your armor before battle, only much more peaceful. By preparing mentally, setting realistic goals, practicing positive imagery, and rehearsing your approach, you equip yourself with the tools to handle social situations not just adequately, but brilliantly. With each event, you'll find yourself becoming more adept at navigating the social seas, turning what once felt like stormy waters into a skilled surf.

Building a Support System: Who to Lean On

Imagine you're trying to build the ultimate cozy place where you can chill, far away from the chaos of the world. You'd want the best materials, right? Well, when it comes to managing social anxiety, your support system is that cozy, safe place. It's made up of people and resources that provide comfort and understanding, helping you navigate the stormy seas of anxiety. Let's start by figuring out how to identify the supportive people in your life and how to strengthen those connections.

Think about the people who make you feel safe. Who comes to mind? Maybe it's a friend who always listens without judgment, a family member who gets it, or a teacher who has a knack for making you feel heard. These are your go-to folks, the pillars of your support system. But it's not just about who is supportive; it's also about nurturing these relationships. The foundation needs to be strong and well-maintained. This means being open about your struggles, expressing gratitude for their support, and being there for them, too. It's a two-way street. By fostering these relationships, you create a network of allies who can stand with you when the going gets tough and cheer you on when you're doing well.

Now, let's talk about peers. It's one thing to have supportive friends, but it's another to have friends who really understand what you're going through because they've been there themselves. These are the friends who can relate to the panic of being called on in class or the dread of social gatherings. Having friends who share similar experiences with social anxiety can be incredibly validating. It reminds you that you're not alone in this. These connections often turn into your front line defense, offering empathy and strategies from their own experiences. They know the battles you face and can provide the specific tactics that have helped them in the past. Plus, as you share your challenges and victories, you'll find strength in numbers, knowing there's a whole squad who's got your back.

Professional help is another cornerstone of a robust support system. There's absolutely no shame in seeking help from counselors or therapists. These professionals can offer guidance tailored to your specific needs. They bring a toolbox of strategies and insights that can help you understand the roots of your anxiety, develop coping mechanisms, and set realistic goals for overcoming your challenges. If you're not sure where to start, a school counselor can be a great resource for finding the help you need.

Online support groups are the broader community of your sanctuary. These platforms connect you with individuals globally who are navigating similar challenges. Through social media groups, forums, and dedicated apps, you gain access to a world where you can exchange stories, glean insights from others' experiences, and discover new coping methods. It's reassuring to witness that you're not alone in your struggles and achievements. However, ensure these spaces are secure and well-moderated to foster a constructive and supportive atmosphere. While online communities are excellent for expanding your circle of support, they should enhance, rather than replace, your direct interactions with friends, family, and professionals.

By building a strong support system, you equip yourself with the best tools and allies to help manage your social anxiety. Whether it's friends who understand, professionals who guide, or communities that uplift, each element of your support network plays a crucial role in your journey toward managing anxiety and thriving despite it. So, take the time to identify and nurture these relationships and resources. They are your safe space, and with them, you'll find the strength to face social challenges more confidently and effectively.

As we wrap up this chapter on building a support system, remember the importance of surrounding yourself with the right people and resources. Your support system is your foundation, offering the strength and stability you need to navigate the complexities of social anxiety. With each person and resource you add, you fortify your ability to cope and grow.

Building and Maintaining Relationships

E ver felt like you're auditioning for a role in the movie of your life, especially when trying to fit into a new social circle? It's like, "Here's me trying to look cool, casual, and collected, all while I'm internally screaming." Let's face it, finding your tribe—the group of people who 'get' you, laugh at your jokes, share your obsessions, or support your dreams —can sometimes feel like searching for a Wi-Fi signal in a desert. But when you do connect, it's nothing short of awesome. This chapter is all about navigating the social jungle to find and cultivate those precious relationships that make you feel like you belong.

Approaching and Finding Your Tribe of Like-Minded Peers

First things first: identifying your interests and passions is like plotting your coordinates on a map. What gets you excited? Video games, books, sports, baking, quantum physics? These aren't just hobbies—they're beacons that attract others who share your enthusiasm. Start by making a list of what you love doing or topics you could talk about all day without getting bored. This list becomes your guide to finding potential friends with similar interests. It's like having a secret password to an exclusive club where everyone shares your passion for anime or your obsession with all things K-pop.

Now that you know what you're into, where do you find these mythical creatures who share your interests? It's time to explore! Schools, community centers, and libraries often host clubs and events centered around different activities like chess, coding, robotics, literature, or drama. These places are your gold mines. Online forums and social media groups can also be fantastic places to connect with like-minded peers globally. Remember, every great explorer had to start somewhere.

Finding your tribe takes initiative. It's easy to think, "If I just sit here long enough, someone will come along," but it's like waiting for a pizza to order itself—it's not going to happen. Take the first step: join the club, post in the forum, attend the gathering. But here's the kicker—be patient. Friendships aren't instant noodles; they don't develop in just five minutes. They need time to simmer and develop. Attend a few meetings or hang out at several events. Let things evolve naturally. Your tribe won't necessarily form overnight, but with a bit of persistence, you'll find your crowd.

Once you've broken the ice and are starting to feel comfortable in a group, it's time to deepen those budding friendships. Moving beyond small talk is your next step. Instead of just chatting about the weather or the latest homework assignment, try sharing a bit about what you're passionate about and ask open-ended questions that encourage others to share their thoughts and feelings. For example, if you're in a book club, instead of just discussing the plot of the book, ask, "How do you think you'd react in a situation like that?" Activities like study groups, weekend hikes, or group projects can also provide perfect opportunities for deeper interactions. These shared experiences create memories and strengthen bonds.

Speaking of shared experiences, they're like the glue that cements relationships. Whether it's working together on a challenging group assignment or attending a concert, doing things together builds camaraderie and trust. Organize activities that resonate with what you and your peers enjoy. From hosting a movie marathon to leading a community clean-up effort, these events are the perfect avenue to bond. They not only provide an opportunity to enjoy each other's company but also help in building a collective memory and cultivating inside jokes—elements that are invaluable in the world of friendship.

Navigating the maze of social interactions to build and maintain relationships might seem daunting, but remember, it's about finding your people—those who share your passions and appreciate your quirks. As you venture out into the social wilds, keep your interests as your compass and your openness as your guide. Before you know it, you'll find yourself surrounded by a tribe that gets you and grows with you.

The Give and Take of Friendships: Maintaining Balance

Navigating the world of friendships is a lot like being a gardener—both require patience, consistent care, and a bit of dirt under your nails from dealing with the messy parts. In friendships, this means having a strong foundation of communication, understanding each other's needs, and balancing your own life with your social connections. Now, let's explore how to nurture your friendships to bloom, even amidst the hustle and bustle of life's demands.

Keeping the spark of friendship alive is akin to watering a precious plant—it requires care, attention, and regular nurturing. It's not merely about catching up; it's about demonstrating your investment and care for the relation-ship. Consistent, even if brief, check-ins play a critical role in sustaining this bond, especially amidst everyone's hectic lives. A simple text like, "Hey, thought of you today!" or "Hope your exam went well!" can convey your thoughts and care, keeping the friendship vibrant and engaged. These small gestures of communication are the threads that strengthen the fabric of your connection, allowing it to endure the tests of time and distance. Thankfully, the digital era offers myriad ways to remain connected. Quick messages or social media DMs are great for sharing laughs or moments as they happen. For a more intimate connection, a video chat or a traditional phone call lets you share your worlds more personally, bridging any physical gap between you. Organizing regular gatherings, such as a monthly movie outing or a study group, creates consistent opportunities to look forward to. Both planned and spontaneous interactions are key to nurturing the roots of your friendship, ensuring it remains strong through life's constant changes.

When you do catch up, being present is key. Active listening isn't just for heart-to-hearts; it's also for those casual chats about everyday stuff. Showing genuine interest in the little details of your friends' lives—like how their sister's birthday party went or their rants about a pet peeve—makes them feel valued. It's not about nodding along but engaging with follow-up questions, empathetic responses, or related stories. This kind of exchange makes each conversation a building block for deeper trust and understanding.

Similar to how each person has a unique taste in music, everyone has their own preferred style of communication. Some friends might love texting and send updates every hour, while others might prefer a catch-up call once a week. Respecting these preferences is crucial—it shows you care about their comfort and boundaries. Pay attention to how they like to communicate and try to meet them on that platform. It's a simple gesture that speaks volumes about your respect for their personal communication style.

Your life isn't just about one friendship or even a group of friends; you've got family, school, hobbies, and maybe even a part-time job in the mix. Keeping a balance can sometimes feel like juggling flaming torches. One useful strategy is integrating your friends with different parts of your life. Maybe study together if you're busy with school, or bring a friend along to a family outing. It's about making quality time, even when quantity isn't feasible. Friendship is a two-way street, with give and take from both sides. Reciprocity isn't about keeping score but ensuring that both of you feel supported and valued. It's noticing when one of you is always initiating plans and conversations and addressing it gently. Maybe your friend isn't aware of it, and a simple conversation can help rebalance the scales. It's about mutual support, where both of you can rely on each other without feeling like one is doing all the heavy lifting.

Your social circle might include friends from different parts of your life—school, sports teams, or online communities. Each friendship is unique and might require different amounts of time and energy. Managing this without feeling stretched thin is key. Be transparent with your friends about your other commitments. Most will understand if you explain why you can't hang out because you've got another obligation. It's about setting realistic expectations and being honest, which most friends will respect. Even the best friendships can hit a snag when feelings of jealousy or competition creep in. Maybe your friend got the lead in the play you both auditioned for, or they started hanging out with a new group, sparking some envy. These feelings are natural, but addressing them openly and honestly can prevent them from festering. Acknowledge your feelings, perhaps in a journal or to another friend, before bringing them up with the person involved. When you do bring it up, focus on your feelings rather than accusing them of wrong-doing. It's about clearing the air and moving forward, not laying blame.

In navigating the complexities of maintaining friendships amidst the whirlwind of teenage life, remember that the effort you put into these relationships is what makes them thrive. Like a garden, friendships require regular tending, but the blooms they produce—trust, support, joy—are well worth the dirt under your nails. So keep communicating, listening, and balancing, and watch as your friendships grow deeper and stronger, providing a stable, joyful presence in your life.

When to Let Go: Navigating the End of a Friendship

So, you've been sailing along the friendship sea, but suddenly, you hit choppy waters. Maybe it's the constant negativity, a lack of support, or even manipulation that's making you seasick. Recognizing when a friendship turns toxic is like spotting a storm on the horizon—it's crucial to acknowledge it before you find yourself in a shipwreck. Toxic relationships can manifest through behaviors that consistently make you feel worse after interactions. If you're frequently feeling drained, disrespected, or devalued, these are your red flags flapping violently in the wind. It's not just about occasional disagreements or rough patches—those are normal in any relationship. Toxicity seeps in when negativity becomes the norm, support turns into sabotage, and manipulation replaces mutual respect.

Handling confrontation in these scenarios isn't about gearing up for battle; it's about setting boundaries with clarity and calmness. Imagine you're drawing a line in the sand—on one side, your well-being; on the other, behaviors you can no longer tolerate. It's important to communicate these boundaries directly. You might say something like, "I feel hurt when my achievements aren't acknowledged. I need us to support each other if our friendship is to continue." This isn't about accusing or blaming, but rather expressing your feelings and defining what you need to remain in the relationship. Sometimes, just being open about your feelings can encourage the other person to reflect and adjust their behavior. However, be prepared for all outcomes. Not everyone will respond positively, but standing up for your emotional needs is a crucial step in nurturing your well-being.

Deciding to distance yourself or end a toxic relationship is a tough call. It's painful, but sometimes necessary to protect your overall health. When you decide it's time to step back or walk away, do so with your mental health as your priority. Communicate your decision respectfully and clearly, without leaving room for ambiguity. "I've given this a lot of thought, and for my well-being, I need to take a step back from our friendship right now," is a way to put it. Ensuring your safety, especially in cases of manipulation or emotional abuse, is paramount. This might mean changing your routines, adjusting privacy settings on social media, or seeking support from other friends or family.

Navigating the emotional aftermath of a friendship breakup can feel like dealing with a mini heartbreak. Whether it's sadness, anger, or even relief, your feelings are valid and need attention. Engage in activities that soothe and reaffirm your worth—like diving into hobbies that bring you joy or spending time with people who uplift you. Self-care strategies like journaling your thoughts, practicing mindfulness, or speaking with a therapist can also help process these emotions. It's about giving yourself the same compassion and support you'd offer a friend in your shoes.

Reflecting on what the experience taught you about relationships can turn a painful ending into a powerful lesson. What red flags might you watch for in the future? What boundaries will you set from the start? Every relationship, even those that end, can teach us something valuable about ourselves and how we relate to others. Perhaps you'll learn about your resilience, or maybe you'll gain clarity on what you truly value in friendships. These insights can guide you in forming healthier, more fulfilling relationships in the future.

If navigating the end of a friendship feels overwhelming, remember, you don't have to go it alone. Reach out for support from friends who understand your value, family members who want to see you happy, or professionals who can provide guidance. Talking it out can lighten your emotional load and reinforce that you're not alone in this. Ending a friendship, especially a toxic one, can sometimes feel like you're losing a part of your world, but it's also an opportunity to rediscover your peace, reclaim your space, and reinvigorate your life with more positive interactions.

Peer Pressure: Standing Firm in Your Values

Imagine you're at a party and someone passes you a drink you really don't want, or your group of friends decides it's hilarious to vandalize a neighborhood sign. Peer pressure—it's like that annoying classmate who won't let you focus. It sneaks into situations, whispering, "Come on, everyone's doing it," making you feel as if stepping out will turn you into social roadkill. But here's the twist: standing up to peer pressure isn't just about saying no; it's about being true to who you are and what you believe in, even when it feels like you're standing in a spotlight at a rock concert—exposed and vulnerable.

First up, let's break down what peer pressure often looks like. It's not always as clear-cut as someone pushing you to try something dangerous. Sometimes, it's subtle—a bunch of friends all agreeing instantly on something you're not cool with, and you feeling the silent weight of their expectations. Whether it's cheating on a test, skipping class, gossiping, or going along with a mean prank, peer pressure can push you to act against your values. Recognizing these moments is the first step to handling them. It's about listening to that gut feeling that whispers, "This isn't right," even if everyone else seems on board.

Now, how do you hold your ground without feeling like you've just declared war on your social life? It starts with assertive communication. This isn't about being aggressive or confrontational, but clearly and calmly stating your position. Practice saying no with confidence. A simple, "Thanks, but I'm good," or, "I don't think that's a great idea," said with a firm tone, can show that you're not up for negotiation. It's about expressing your stance without apology—owning your no as much as you'd own a yes.

But let's be real, sometimes the pressure can feel like a tidal wave, and standing against it can feel daunting. This is where having a backup can make all the difference. Lean on your support system—friends who share your values, a trusted adult, or even a mentor. Discussing these scenarios with them can bolster your resolve and remind you that you're not alone in wanting to stick to your guns. They can offer that crucial morale boost, or even advice based on their own battles with peer pressure.

Role-play Exercises: Practicing Your Stand

Role-playing can be a powerful tool to prepare for real-life scenarios. Grab a friend or family member and rehearse some of the situations where you might face peer pressure. Have them play the part of the peer pressurer, and practice responding assertively. These rehearsals can be fun—maybe even throw in some ridiculous peer pressure scenarios to lighten the mood. It's like dress rehearsal for a play; the more you practice, the more confident you'll feel when the actual situation arises.

Lastly, aligning your actions with your personal values is perhaps the most empowering defense against peer pressure. Spend some time reflecting on what matters most to you. What are your non-negotiables? What lines will you not cross, no matter who's pressuring you? Writing these down can solidify them in your mind.

Navigating the tricky waters of peer pressure is about knowing yourself, asserting yourself, and sometimes, yes, extricating yourself from toxic situations. But remember, every time you stand firm against peer pressure, you're not just saying no to something you don't want to do—you're saying yes to yourself, to your values, and to the person you are growing to be. So, own your decisions, lean on your support, and keep rehearsing your best moves. You've got this, and with each stand, you're not just surviving the social pressures—you're thriving through them.

Empathy: Understanding and Connecting with Others' Feelings

Empathy might just be the superglue that holds relationships together. Think of it like having a versatile tool that helps you connect with others on a deeper level. It allows you to understand their feelings and perspectives, improving communication and strengthening relationships. Just as a skilled craftsman uses different tools for different tasks, empathy lets you navigate various social situations with understanding and care. But what exactly is empathy? It's not just about feeling sorry for someone; it's about connecting with their feelings, understanding their perspective as if you were in their shoes, not just looking at them.

So, how do you pump up your empathy muscles? It starts with active listening, which is like tuning into a radio frequency that picks up everything, not just the words but the emotions and nuances behind them. When a friend is talking about how they bombed a presentation, listen to the disappointment in their voice, watch their body language—maybe they're fidgeting or looking down. These signals tell you more about how they're feeling than their words might say. Next, level up your empathy game by asking questions that show you're really engaged. Instead of a generic "That sucks," try "What part of the presentation threw you off?" This shows you're not just hearing them but are genuinely interested in understanding their experience.

But it's not just about listening and asking questions; it's also about reading nonverbal cues. Much of what we communicate is through body language, facial expressions, and even our silences. Sharpening your ability to read these signs can give you deeper insights into what someone is really feeling. For instance, if someone says they're "fine" but won't meet your eyes, or their smile doesn't quite reach their eyes, these are clues that they might be anything but fine.

Why bother with all this? Because empathy has the power to transform your relationships. It builds trust and respect, showing your friends and even acquaintances that you value their feelings and experiences. When people feel understood, they're more likely to open up and share more deeply, creating a stronger bond. It's about creating a safe space where friends can be honest and vulnerable, knowing they won't be judged or dismissed. This kind of supportive environment can be the foundation for lasting friendships and even help mend bridges that might have been damaged by misunderstandings or conflicts.

Empathy also smooths out the rough edges in relationships. It's easy to get annoyed if your friend is always late or constantly texting when you're hanging out. But if you take a moment to think about what might be causing their behavior —maybe they're going through a tough time and aren't even aware of how it's affecting them—it can change how you respond. Instead of getting irritated, you might offer to help them figure out a better schedule or find time to really talk about what's going on. Just like that, empathy turns what could be a conflict into a moment of connection.

Of course, empathy isn't just for the easy times; it's crucial when the going gets tough. When you're in the middle of a disagreement, empathy allows you to see the other person's point of view, even if you don't agree with it. This can be a game-changer. It's the difference between a shouting match that ends with slammed doors and a conversation that leads to a mutual understanding, even if the only agreement is to disagree. And when you don't fully understand someone's perspective—maybe your backgrounds are too different, or their experiences are far removed from your own— empathy encourages you to ask questions and keep an open mind, rather than jumping to conclusions or making assumptions.

So, whether you're dealing with a friend's bad day, a family disagreement, or just trying to connect better with the people around you, think of empathy as your go-to tool. It's not always easy to put yourself in someone else's shoes—to really tune into their feelings and perspectives—but the effort is worth it. Because at the end of the day, empathy not only makes your relationships stronger, but it also makes you a more compassionate and understanding person. And in a world that could use a little more understanding, that's no small thing.

Sharing and Respecting Boundaries

Imagine you're at a concert, right in the middle of the crowd. The music's great, but everyone's a bit too close for comfort. Personal space? Nonexistent. It's the same with relationships; without clear boundaries, things can get uncomfortable fast. Understanding and setting personal boundaries isn't about building walls around yourself; it's more like drawing a map that shows others where they can and can't go. It's about knowing where your limits lie and respecting those of others, ensuring everyone can enjoy the concert, so to speak, without getting elbowed in the face.

So, what exactly are personal boundaries? They're the guidelines or limits we set with other people, which determine acceptable behaviors, responsibilities, and actions. Boundaries can be about anything: your time, your emotions, your personal space, or your energy. They're crucial because they protect your well-being and sense of self-respect, and they help you manage how you interact with others. Think of them as rules of engagement that ensure mutual respect and appreciation. For example, if you're not a fan of last-minute plans, a boundary might be requiring a heads-up at least a day in advance. This keeps your stress levels in check and lets your friends know how to respect your time.

Setting these boundaries clearly and respectfully is key. It starts with self-reflection. Understand what you're comfortable with, what you value, and what you need to stay emotionally and physically healthy. Are you okay with your friend borrowing your clothes but not your phone? Do you need quiet time after school to decompress? These are boundaries, and they're personal to you. Communicating them effectively involves being direct and honest. You might say something like, "I love helping you study, but I need to do it on weekends instead of school nights. Is that cool?" This kind of clear, respectful communication can prevent misunderstandings and build trust within your relationships.

Respecting others' boundaries is just as crucial. Pay attention to verbal cues and body language. If a friend steps back when you're in their personal space, or changes the subject when you bring up a sensitive topic, these are hints. They might not always say it outright, but it's important to be observant and sensitive to these signals. If you're unsure, it's okay to ask. A simple, "Is this okay with you?" can go a long way. This shows that you respect their comfort levels and are willing to adjust your behavior to maintain a healthy relationship.

Dealing with boundary violations is something most of us will face at some point. If someone repeatedly ignores your boundaries, it's essential to address the issue directly. Reaffirm your boundaries with a firm yet respectful tone. Let them know how their actions affect you and reiterate your limits. You might need to say, "I mentioned before that I need two days' notice to make plans. It's important for me to manage my schedule and keep stress low. Can we make sure this happens next time?" If the behavior continues, it might be necessary to evaluate the health of the relationship and consider distancing yourself to protect your well-being.

Navigating personal boundaries is a continuous process of communication, respect, and mutual understanding. It's about giving yourself and others the space to feel safe and respected. By setting and respecting boundaries, you're not just taking care of yourself; you're also fostering healthier, more balanced relationships that allow everyone to flourish.

Supporting Friends During Tough Times

Sometimes being a friend feels like being a superhero without the flashy cape, especially when someone you care about hits a rough patch. You know, those times when a friend seems more 'meh' than 'yeah!' and you can't help but worry? Spotting these signs early can make all the difference. Maybe they're texting less, or their laugh doesn't quite reach their eyes anymore. Perhaps they're pulling away from the group, ditching plans, or just seem off. These are your cues that they might need a friend to step in, not to save the day, but to show they're not alone.

Now, offering help can be tricky; it's like trying to figure out the right amount of sugar in your friend's coffee—too little, and it's bitter, too much and it's undrinkable. The key is to offer support in a way that feels respectful and appropriate. Start by simply being there. Sometimes, you don't need to do anything spectacular. Just showing up, being present, can speak volumes. Listen to them, really listen, without distractions or the urge to fix everything right away. Often, what your friend needs is to feel heard and understood, not immediately offered solutions or advice.

Maintaining this supportive presence is like keeping your phone charged; it requires consistent effort. Check in regularly, and not just when things seem bad. Send a message, share a meme, or drop by with their favorite snack. Small gestures show that you care and are there for them, not just for the drama but for the long haul. It's about building a safety net of trust and care, so they know they can count on you when the going gets tough. And remember, being supportive also means respecting their journey and their timetable. Everyone heals and copes differently, and that's okay.

Encouraging professional help is delicate territory. It's like suggesting someone see a doctor for a physical injury that won't heal. If you feel your friend's struggles are bigger than what friends and family can support—like dealing with persistent sadness, anxiety, or any behavior that significantly impacts their life—it might be time to suggest professional help. Approach this conversation with care. Start by expressing your concern and your unconditional support. You might say, "I've noticed you've been feeling really down. It might be helpful to talk to someone who can provide more support than I can. I really care about you and want you to feel better." Ensure they understand that seeking help is a sign of strength, not weakness. Offer to help them find a therapist or even go with them to the first appointment if they're nervous.

Navigating the stormy waters of a friend's tough times isn't about being a hero; it's about being a friend—someone who stands by, offers a shoulder, and respects their process. It's about showing that no matter how fierce the storm, they don't have to weather it alone.

Dealing with Conflicts: Effective Strategies for Teens

Navigating the choppy waters of teen conflicts is kind of like trying to solve a Rubik's cube—it can be super frustrating, but oh-so-satisfying when you finally get the colors to line up. Conflicts are a normal part of growing up and forging relationships. They're not just about clashing over whose turn it is on the Xbox or disagreements over group project roles; they're valuable opportunities to develop your communication chops, empathy, and problem-solving skills.

Spotting the early signs of conflict is like catching a cold before it turns into a full-blown flu—you can manage it more effectively with early intervention. Pay attention to the vibe between you and your friends. Are your usual jokes not landing well? Is there more eye-rolling than smiling going on? These could be early warning signals that not everything is cool. Addressing these signs early can prevent a molehill

from turning into a mountain. Just bringing up your observations can help, like saying, "Hey, I noticed we've been a bit
off lately. Is there something on your mind?" It shows you're
aware and care about keeping things smooth.

When it comes to the crunch, how you talk can make or
break a resolution. Steering through a conflict with grace
involves clear, calm, and respectful communication. Using "I"
statements can be a game-changer here. Instead of accusing
or blaming, which can put your friend on defense, speak
from your perspective: "I feel left out when plans are made
without telling me." It's like saying, "Here's my side of the
story," without pointing fingers. Listening is just as crucial.
Give your friend space to express their side and really listen
—no planning your counter-attack while they speak. This
two-way street approach can lead to more understanding
and less drama.

Let's face it, seeing eye to eye on everything is impossible,
and that's okay. Finding a middle ground, where each person
gives a little to get a little, often saves the day. Compromise
doesn't mean you're losing; it means you're prioritizing
peace and the relationship over winning an argument.
Maybe you agree to alternate choices in your hangout spots
or find a group project role that suits each person's
strengths. This isn't just about bending to make peace; it's
about crafting a solution that everyone can live with, keeping
the friendship on solid ground.

So, you've navigated through the storm, and things are
starting to calm down. Now what? Restoring and even
strengthening your friendship post-conflict is crucial. A
simple, sincere talk about how much you value their friend-

ship can mend fences and reinforce your bond. Maybe plan something fun together, like a movie night or trying out a new coffee shop or restaurant—something that reminds you both why you're friends in the first place. It's about moving forward with a renewed commitment to your friendship, now fortified by overcoming a challenge together.

Sometimes, conflicts can get too tangled to unravel on your own. If you find yourself feeling overwhelmed, or if the conflict is affecting your mental health, reaching out for help is a wise move. A counselor, a trusted teacher, or another adult can provide guidance, mediate the situation, and offer new perspectives. There's no shame in seeking help; it shows you're mature enough to recognize when a situation is beyond your current toolkit.

Navigating conflicts effectively requires a blend of self-awareness, communication skills, and emotional intelligence. By recognizing signs early, communicating effectively, seeking compromise, and sometimes getting help, you equip yourself not just to handle conflicts but to emerge from them with stronger, more resilient relationships. Remember, every conflict is a chance to learn more about yourself and others. With these strategies in hand, you're better prepared to face and resolve conflicts, ensuring they lead to growth instead of grudges.

Remember that these experiences are part of your journey toward becoming a more empathetic and effective communicator. Conflicts, when navigated wisely, can deepen understanding and strengthen bonds. Keep these tools ready, and you'll be more equipped to turn potential confrontations into opportunities for growth and connection.

Make a Difference with your Review

"The key to being a great conversationalist is to genuinely care about what others have to say."

— Unknown

Hey there, awesome reader!

We hope you're enjoying "Unlocking Social Skills for Teens" by Kimberly Myrick so far! Just like showing your creative side on Instagram or your clever thoughts on Twitter, this book is here to help you shine in real-life social situations.

There are teens out there just like you, trying to overcome social anxiety, feeling unsure, and looking for guidance. Your review could be the thing that helps them find this book and start their journey.

Your review is free and takes less than 60 seconds, but it can have a huge impact. Your words might help another teen:

- Feel more confident in social situations.
- Make new friends.
- Learn important skills that will help them for life.

To leave your review, simply scan the QR code below:

Thank you from the bottom of our hearts. Keep up the great work and enjoy the rest of the book!

Your biggest fan,

Kimberly Myrick

Navigating Complex Social Settings

Ever felt like high school is a safari, and you're wandering through it without a map? One minute you're dodging the 'lions' (hello, senior year exams), the next you're trying to blend in with the 'camouflage experts' (those groups that seem to have it all figured out). Welcome to the wild world of school social hierarchies, where knowing your way around can make the difference between thriving and merely surviving. But fear not! This chapter is your GPS through this social jungle, helping you find your place, connect with diverse groups, and handle the pressures that come with the territory—all without losing your cool or your unique self.

School Social Hierarchies: Finding Your Place

First up, let's decode what a social hierarchy even is. In every school, like in every pack of animals, there's an unspoken order—a set of social ranks that students navigate daily. These hierarchies can be based on various things: popularity, academic achievements, athletic ability, or even extracurricular involvement. Recognizing this pecking order is kind of like identifying the rules of a game. Once you know what influences these ranks, you can better understand where you fit and how you can navigate this landscape smartly.

Knowing your spot in this social hierarchy isn't about resigning yourself to a 'rank' but about understanding how to navigate these waters with your authenticity intact. Start by observing. Who are the influencers? What values seem to matter in your school's social economy? Is it sports prowess, artistic talent, or something else? Understanding this can help you identify not just where you fit, but also how you can connect authentically with different groups. Remember, this isn't about changing who you are—it's about understanding the terrain and choosing your paths wisely.

Now, about mingling with the masses—integrating into various groups doesn't mean losing your values or playing a part. It's about finding common ground. Start small. Participate in activities that align with your interests and offer opportunities to interact with different people. It could be joining a sports team, the school play, or the debate club. These platforms can serve as neutral territories where different social circles overlap. When you share activities, conversations often flow easier, and genuine connections can form without the pressure of fitting into a predefined 'slot'.

Friendships that bridge different social groups are like having feet in two different worlds—they enrich your perspective and can often redefine boundaries. Cultivate these friendships by focusing on individual relationships rather than group affiliations. Be the one who greets everyone, regardless of their 'group.' When you're known as someone who doesn't stick to one clique, you naturally become a social connector, reducing the impact of rigid hierarchies. Plus, these friendships can be your safe harbors when social seas get choppy.

Pressure to conform can be intense, especially when it feels like everyone else has it figured out. Here's where you need to tune into your own values and boundaries. It's okay to say no, to decline an invite, or to stand up for something you believe in. Sometimes, the simple act of expressing your own views can earn you respect from others, even if they don't share your perspective. If the pressure gets overwhelming, don't hesitate to reach out for support—whether it's talking to a trusted teacher, counselor, or a good friend.

No one likes feeling like the odd one out. If you find yourself on the outskirts, or if the clique culture is getting you down, take a proactive approach. Look for others who might also be feeling left out, or start a new group centered around an interest or hobby. Creating an inclusive space not only provides a refuge for those who feel marginalized but also challenges the clique culture by modeling inclusivity.

Navigating the complex social settings of school requires a mix of observation, genuine engagement, and a firm sense of self. By understanding the social landscape, integrating wisely, building bridges across groups, and handling pressures with grace, you can navigate through your school years not just as a survivor but as a savvy explorer. Remember, every interaction is a step in learning more about others and about yourself. So keep your eyes open, your mind sharp, and your heart open—the social safari is always full of surprises.

Seeking Feedback: How to Use Criticism Constructively

Ever felt like feedback is the school cafeteria's mystery meat —hard to swallow, and you're not always sure if it's good for you? Yet, just like that questionable lunch, feedback is pretty essential. It's the secret sauce that can spice up your social skills and help you grow. But to really benefit from it, you need to develop a taste for feedback, even when it's served a bit raw. Let's break down how you can take criticism and turn it into your superpower, making it less of a bitter pill and more of a growth tonic.

Think of feedback not as a personal attack, but as a cheat sheet that helps you level up. It's important to stay open and not let your defenses shoot up like a prickly cactus every time someone has a suggestion for you. Remember, when people offer you feedback, it's not because they want to watch you squirm—it's usually because they believe you can reach higher grounds. To keep your cool, take a deep breath and remind yourself that everyone, even the most seemingly perfect people, have room for improvement. Think of it as being in a video game where feedback is the bonus tool that helps boost your stats.

Now, getting useful feedback isn't just about standing there and taking whatever comes your way. You've got to be proactive and ask for it like you're mining for gold. When you ask for feedback, be specific about what you want to improve. Instead of a generic "How am I doing?" try

"What's one thing I could change about how I contribute in group discussions?" This gives the other person a clear target and shows you're serious about self-improvement. Also, timing is key. Ask for feedback right after a specific event or situation while it's still fresh in everyone's mind. This way, you get detailed, actionable insights instead of vague memories.

Once you've got the feedback, the next step is to sift through it like you're panning for gold—keep the nuggets and let the rest wash away. Not all feedback will be useful, and that's okay. Evaluate what aligns with your goals and what doesn't. If your math teacher suggests you need to speak up more in class, but your goal is to improve your written work, prioritize the feedback that matches your objectives. When you decide which pieces of advice to act on, break them down into small, manageable steps. This could mean setting personal challenges, like asking at least two questions in each class session or offering to help a classmate with a difficult problem.

While it's great to get outside perspectives, don't forget to check in with yourself. After all, you're the captain of your ship. Regularly take some time to reflect on your own perceptions of your social interactions. Maybe journal about a recent group project or a social event and rate how you think you did. Then, compare your notes with the feedback you received. This can help you spot patterns, like maybe you're tougher on yourself than you need to be, or perhaps there's a blind spot you hadn't noticed. Balancing these internal and external inputs helps you develop a well-rounded view of your social skills and guides you in setting realistic, personal growth goals.

By turning feedback into a tool for growth rather than a source of stress, you empower yourself to actively shape your social abilities. Whether it's fine-tuning your conversation skills or boosting your confidence, every piece of advice you choose to implement is a stepping stone towards becoming a more adept, resilient social navigator. So keep seeking out those golden nuggets of feedback, and watch as your social skills transform, one constructive critique at a time.

Family Gatherings: Interacting with Different Generations

Attending family gatherings can often resemble navigating a complex cultural mosaic, where each age group brings its own set of traditions, expectations, and ways of communicating. But fear not! Bridging the generation gap doesn't require a peace treaty—just a sprinkle of patience, a dash of empathy, and a good understanding of how to communicate across different age groups. Whether it's decoding your grandpa's tales from 'the good old days' or explaining to your little cousin why your phone isn't just for making calls, finding common ground can turn a regular family gathering into a mini adventure in bonding.

Communicating effectively with both older and younger family members is all about showing genuine interest in their lives. With older relatives, this might mean asking about their experiences and really listening (yes, even if you've heard the story a hundred times). It shows respect and appreciation for their wisdom and journey. On the flip side, connecting with younger cousins or siblings often means stepping into their world. Maybe it's playing a video game with them or asking about their favorite TikTok trends. By engaging with their interests, you're building bridges on their terms, which can be both enlightening and fun.

While it's great to dive into these different worlds, balancing this with being true to yourself is key. Family gatherings often come with a hearty side of tradition, and while traditions can be wonderful, they can also be a bit stifling if you feel like you can't express your own views or preferences. The trick is to respect the traditions while also weaving in your own individuality. For instance, if your family's traditional holiday dinner feels outdated, suggest a new dish that you love. It's a simple way to introduce something new without tossing out the cherished old, showing that traditions can evolve and include everyone's tastes.

When it comes to engaging in family conversations, it's like being a conductor of an orchestra where every instrument matters. Whether it's a heated debate about politics or a discussion about where to go for your next family vacation, contributing in a way that acknowledges and respects all viewpoints can turn chaotic discussions into harmonious dialogues. Start by acknowledging the points made before you add your perspective. This not only shows respect but also keeps the conversation inclusive and flowing smoothly. Remember, the goal isn't to win an argument but to share ideas and learn from each other, strengthening family bonds in the process.

Handling intrusive questions from relatives, like "How's school going?" or "Are you seeing anyone?" can sometimes make you wish for invisibility superpowers. But since cloaking devices are still not a family dinner option, crafting tactful responses is your next best strategy. Prepare polite but vague answers that satisfy curiosity without divulging too much. For example, "School's going well, I'm learning a lot!" or "I'm happy focusing on myself right now." Such responses keep the peace and protect your privacy without offending the asker.

Lastly, dealing with family conflicts without turning dinner into a drama series involves a good dose of neutrality and stress management. When tensions rise, strive to stay neutral and avoid taking sides. If a conflict escalates, suggest discussing the issue at another time when everyone's calmer, or excuse yourself politely if things get too heated. Remember, sometimes stepping away gracefully is the best way to maintain peace and your own sanity.

Family gatherings, with their blend of ages, personalities, and traditions, are unique opportunities to strengthen ties and create new memories. By effectively bridging the generation gap, respecting traditions while being yourself, contributing thoughtfully to conversations, handling sensitive questions with tact, and managing conflicts with poise, you can navigate these gatherings with confidence and maybe even enjoy the chaos a little. After all, at the end of the day, family is a lot like fudge—mostly sweet with a few nuts, and always better when shared.

Public Speaking: Gaining Confidence and Overcoming Anxiety

Does the mere thought of standing in front of a crowd make your stomach do somersaults? You're not alone. Public speaking is often ranked as one of the top fears, right up there with skydiving into a pit of spiders. But why this widespread dread? At its core, the fear of public speaking, also known as glossophobia, often stems from the worry of being judged. You're putting yourself out there, and the possibility of stumbling over your words or drawing a blank can feel like walking a tightrope without a net. Another common fear factor is the worry of not being prepared enough, which can send your mind into a tailspin of 'what ifs.'

Overcoming these fears starts with changing your perspective. Think of public speaking not as a performance, but as a conversation with a friend. You're just sharing something you know or care about with a few more friends than usual. This mindset shift can take the edge off the intimidation and help you focus more on the message rather than on the fear of how it's received.

When it comes to tackling nervousness head-on, preparation is your best ally. Start by organizing your thoughts. Create a clear outline of your speech with a strong opening, informative middle, and a memorable conclusion. Knowing exactly what you want to say and when to say it can boost your confidence and reduce anxiety. Practice, and then practice some more—out loud and in front of a mirror or a supportive friend. The more familiar you are with your speech, the less likely you'll be thrown off by nerves or distractions on the big day.

But let's not forget about those jitters on the day of the speech. Here's where those relaxation strategies that we've discussed before come into play. Deep breathing exercises can be a lifesaver. It helps reduce anxiety by increasing the amount of oxygen in your brain and relaxing your muscles. Also, visualization can be used as a powerful tool here. Picture yourself delivering a successful speech. Imagine the applause and the feeling of accomplishment. This positive visual reinforcement can be a huge confidence booster.

Now, structuring your speech for impact is crucial. Start strong with a hook—an interesting fact, a question, or a compelling story to grab attention. Organize your points logically so that your audience can easily follow along, and end with a call to action or a thought-provoking statement that leaves a lasting impression. Throughout your speech, remember to engage with your audience. Make eye contact, ask rhetorical questions, or include short pauses to let important points sink in. These techniques can help maintain interest and make your speech more interactive.

Finally, nothing beats real-world practice. Join clubs or groups like debate teams or drama clubs where public speaking is a regular activity. These platforms offer a safe space to hone your skills, receive constructive feedback, and gradually build your confidence in front of an audience. Every opportunity to speak publicly is a chance to improve, learn from feedback, and diminish the fear associated with public speaking.

By embracing these strategies, you can transform public speaking from a nerve-wracking chore into an exciting opportunity to share your thoughts and ideas. Remember, every speaker started somewhere, and every opportunity to speak is a step forward in your journey to becoming a confident, effective communicator. So take a deep breath, visualize your success, and step up to the podium. Your audience is waiting.

Group Projects: Collaborating Effectively

When you think about group projects, you might feel like you're either about to engage in an epic team-up like in a superhero movie or you're being thrown into a lion's den where everyone is fighting for the last piece of meat. But hey, group projects don't have to be a dreaded ordeal. They're actually a fantastic playground to sharpen your social and collaborative skills, and who knows, you might just end up making some great friends along the way!

Diving into a group project is a bit like starting a band. You wouldn't have everyone playing the drums and nobody on vocals, right? Similarly, defining clear roles and responsibilities in a group project sets the stage for a smooth performance. The key here is to ensure that everyone has a part that suits their strengths and interests. Have a chat with your group members to discuss each person's skills and how they align with the project needs. Maybe you're great at research, while someone else excels at graphic design or presentation skills. Matching roles to skills boosts the group's efficiency and makes the work more enjoyable for everyone. But remember, fair doesn't always mean equal: some roles might require more work than others, so be ready to balance the workload by negotiating responsibilities that feel right to everyone involved.

As with any relationship, communication is the cornerstone of effective collaboration. Think of your group as a mini-team, and your project's success depends on how well this team communicates. Establish regular check-ins where everyone shares updates, challenges, and next steps. Tools like group chats or collaborative platforms can keep the conversation flowing and documents accessible to all members. But it's not just about updating each other; it's also about being open and honest. If you're feeling overwhelmed or stuck, say it. If you think the project is veering off track, speak up. Constructive communication helps nip potential issues in the bud and keeps everyone on the same page.

Here's the not-so-fun part: conflicts happen. Different opinions and working styles can clash, and without careful handling, these clashes can turn ugly. When tensions rise, keep the focus on the project's goals rather than personal differences. Encourage everyone to express their views respectfully and look for compromises where possible. Sometimes, just understanding the reasoning behind a teammate's perspective can turn a conflict into a constructive discussion. And if you're the mediator, remember to stay neutral; think of yourself as a referee in a friendly game, not taking sides but making sure everyone plays fair.

There's almost always that one group member who doesn't pull their weight, and dealing with them can be frustrating. Start by addressing the issue directly but diplomatically. Sometimes, people aren't aware of the impact of their actions until it's pointed out. A simple conversation explaining how their lack of participation is affecting the group might nudge them to step up. If the behavior continues, it might be time to involve a teacher or project advisor. They can offer additional support or intervention to help realign the team's efforts. Remember, the goal is to keep the project on track, not to create a villain out of the non-cooperative member.

Navigating group projects is a lot like mastering a complex dance. It takes coordination, clear communication, and a fair bit of patience. But with each project, you'll find yourself becoming more adept at working with others, handling unexpected challenges, and leading collective efforts toward a common goal. So, embrace the chaos, find your rhythm, and let the collaborative magic happen. Who knows? This could be the beginning of some beautiful academic friendships or, at the very least, a stellar project grade!

Navigating Social Gatherings: Mingling, Safety, and Making Connections

Stepping into a social gathering can sometimes feel like you're about to perform a high-wire act without a net. The lights, the crowd, the noise—it's all exhilarating and, let's be honest, a bit nerve-wracking. But with the right mental prep, you can turn that anxiety into excitement and truly shine. Think of each gathering as a mini-adventure. Before you dive in, it's smart to scout out the terrain. Understanding the venue and the host, getting a vibe of the guest list, and knowing what's expected in terms of behavior and attire can make you feel more at ease. It's like knowing the rules of a game before you start playing. If it's a casual get-together at a friend's house, your favorite hoodie might be perfect. But if it's a more formal event, you might want to swap the hoodie for something a bit sharper. Doing your homework means you won't stick out like a sore thumb, and it gives you a confidence boost knowing you're well-prepared.

Let's talk about tackling crowded settings. It's all fun and games until you find yourself in the middle of a packed room, feeling more like you're in a can of sardines than at a party. The key here is to maintain your composure. Take deep breaths to keep the internal panic at bay. Position yourself at the edges of larger groups where the sea parts a bit, making it easier to join conversations without feeling overwhelmed. And remember, there's no rule saying you have to plunge into the crowd. Sometimes, standing back and observing can give you a good read on the room's dynamics before you dive in.

Feeling overwhelmed is perfectly normal, especially in lively or crowded events. If the buzz becomes too much, give yourself permission to take a breather. Step outside for some fresh air or find a quieter corner to regroup. These little pauses can recharge your social batteries and help you manage sensory overload. It's like hitting the reset button—when you step back into the fray, you'll likely feel more centered and ready to mingle.

Safety should always be your top priority. Stick with your squad, especially in unfamiliar settings or large crowds. There's safety in numbers, and it's always good to have a few trusted friends who can watch your back. Also, have a plan for getting home safely. Whether it's arranging a ride-share or confirming who's driving, knowing how you're getting home can ease a lot of anxiety. And, of course, always trust your gut. If something feels off, it probably is. Don't be afraid to leave a situation that doesn't feel right.

Peer pressure can sneak up on you, especially in settings where the vibe feels like "anything goes." Be prepared to stand your ground. If you're offered a drink or invited to partake in something that doesn't sit right with you, a firm "no thanks" is your best defense. Practice saying it without apology. Remember, true friends will respect your choices, no matter what.

Navigating social gatherings is a mix of preparation, self-awareness, and a bit of social savvy. With these strategies in your back pocket, you can dive into any social setting with confidence. Remember, each interaction is an opportunity to learn, connect, and grow. So, take a deep breath, put on your best smile, and get ready to make some memorable connections.

Joining and Exiting Group Conversations

Navigating the choppy waters of group conversations can sometimes feel like you're a DJ trying to mix tracks that don't quite sync up. You know, one track is the chill vibes from your study group, and the other is the high-energy beats from your soccer team buddies. Finding the right moment to jump into the conversation mix without scratching the record requires a keen sense of timing and a good read of the room's dynamics. Start by observing the group's body language and the flow of the conversation. Are they leaning in, animated with hands flying everywhere, or are they more laid-back, each person politely taking their turn? This can give you clues about when it might be a good time to chime in. If you see an opening, like a pause in the conversation or someone asking a question that you know the answer to, those are your cues to step up to the turntables.

Once you're in, how do you make sure you're adding value and not just noise? It's all about building on what's already there. Maybe someone just shared a story about their weekend hiking trip. Jumping in with a related experience or a thoughtful question can keep the conversation flowing and show that you're engaged. If you're bringing up a new topic, try to tie it back to something that was discussed earlier. For example, if the group was talking about favorite movies, and you want to switch to books, you might say, "Speaking of movies, has anyone read a book recently that they think would make a great movie?" This way, your transition feels smooth, not jarring, keeping the beat going.

Mixing social circles at gatherings can be like trying to blend different music genres—it can go really well or... not. When introducing friends from different circles, find common ground that they can connect over. Maybe they both love vintage comic books or they're both into indie music. Highlight these shared interests when you introduce them, which can help set the stage for a new friendship. And remember, as the mutual friend, your role is to facilitate the conversation initially but also to step back when appropriate, allowing the new connection to grow.

Knowing when to exit a group conversation gracefully is just as crucial as knowing when to enter. Watch for cues like the conversation winding down or shifting to a topic you're not involved in. You can bow out with a polite, "I'll let you guys chat about that—I'm going to grab some more snacks, see you in a bit!" or "I need to catch up with someone before they leave, it was great chatting!" These kinds of statements signal that you're leaving without making it awkward, maintaining social smoothness.

Being a gracious guest extends beyond just conversations. It includes knowing what to bring to an event, how to thank your host, and how to conduct yourself throughout the gathering. Always ask the host if you can bring anything—this shows consideration and helps ease the host's load. A thank you at the end of the event, whether in person or a follow-up message, goes a long way in showing appreciation. And throughout the event, be mindful of your behavior. Help out where needed, engage politely with other guests, and respect the venue and its rules. These gestures make you a guest that hosts love to invite back, ensuring your social DJ skills are always in demand, ready to mix the perfect social soundtrack wherever you go.

New School and Joining Extracurricular Activities

Imagine stepping into a new school or joining a fresh club— it's like being the new character in a season of your favorite show. Everyone's curious about you, and you're trying to figure out your role in this exciting new plot. This is your chance to script your own epic school year, and it all starts with building new relationships. When you're the newbie, sparking connections might feel a bit like trying to start a fire without matches. But don't worry, you've got this! Begin by finding common interests. It could be that you and a classmate are both into the latest TikTok trend or maybe you overhear someone raving about a book you love. Jump into these conversations with genuine curiosity. Ask questions, share your thoughts, and let your enthusiasm show. People are drawn to passion, and this can be your bridge to new friendships.

Now, about navigating those tricky school or club politics. Every group has its own set of unspoken rules and hierarchies—it's like stepping onto a new game board. The key here is to observe and learn. Watch how members interact, who takes the lead, and how decisions are made. This isn't about plotting a takeover; it's about understanding the dynamics so you can navigate them smartly. Stay true to your values and find ways to fit in without fading into the background. For instance, if you're in a club where senior members dominate, look for opportunities to contribute in ways that highlight your strengths, like suggesting a new project idea or volunteering to manage part of an event.

Engaging in extracurricular activities is not just about filling your afternoon schedule; it's about sculpting your social skills and expanding your network. Whether it's sports, debate, drama, or robotics, each activity offers a unique set of skills and experiences. Sports teams teach you about teamwork and resilience under pressure, debate clubs enhance your argumentative skills and boost confidence, while drama groups can improve your public speaking and empathy by putting you in someone else's shoes. Choose activities that not only interest you but also challenge you to grow.

Participation is more than just showing up; it's about being actively involved. If you're in a club, don't just be another face in the crowd. Volunteer for roles that allow you to show leadership and initiative, like organizing an event or leading a team project. These roles can increase your visibility and impact within the group, making you a valued member. Engage in discussions, offer help, and be reliable. When people see you as someone who contributes positively, they're more likely to respect and include you.

Balancing these activities with your academic and social life can be like juggling fire sticks—you want to keep everything in the air without getting burned. It's crucial to manage your time wisely. Use a planner or digital app to keep track of your commitments and make sure you have time for schoolwork, activities, and some downtime. Remember, quality trumps quantity. It's better to be fully committed to a few activities than to stretch yourself too thin across many.

Let's talk real-life examples. Consider someone like Alex, a high school sophomore who joined the swim team and the school newspaper. Initially overwhelmed, Alex started using a planner to allocate time for practices, meets, interviews, and writing articles. By communicating openly with coaches and editors about his schedule, Alex not only managed his responsibilities but also excelled. His active participation led to him becoming a team captain and a chief editor, roles that honed his leadership skills and built lasting friendships.

In the whirlwind of new schools and activities, remember that each step you take, every new person you meet, and every challenge you overcome is shaping you into a more capable, confident individual. So dive into these experiences with an open heart and a strategic mind. The skills and relationships you build here are more than just resume additions; they're stepping stones to your future.

How Volunteering Expands Your Social Skills

Diving into volunteer work is like stepping into a mini-society where every interaction and task can help polish your people skills, and you come out not just with a sense of accomplishment but also with a toolkit brimming with new abilities. Volunteering naturally places you in situations where you meet a kaleidoscope of people—different ages, backgrounds, and life stories. This melting pot of perspectives isn't just interesting; it's a goldmine for boosting your empathy. Imagine helping out at a community kitchen or a charity run; you're not just serving food or handing out water bottles, you're connecting with a wide array of human experiences, each interaction adding a layer to your understanding of others.

These encounters are more than just passing moments; they're lessons in human dynamics. You learn to read the room, sense moods, and adapt your approach to different people. It's like having real-life emojis flashing above people's heads, showing you what approach works best. This heightened sense of empathy not only makes you a better volunteer but also a more considerate friend, sibling, and classmate. It's the kind of skill that spills over into every area of your life, enriching your interactions and deepening your relationships.

Transitioning to the specific skills that volunteering can bolster, we delve into communication, leadership, and teamwork—three pillars of interpersonal competence. Whether you're guiding visitors at a museum, organizing a fundraising event, or leading a team of fellow volunteers in a community project, each role demands a specific set of skills. Communication becomes key when you have to explain tasks, convey messages clearly, or cheer on your team. Leadership comes into play when you're tasked with coordinating a group or taking the lead on a project. Suddenly, you're the captain of the ship, steering your crew through the seas of tasks and deadlines.

And let's not forget about teamwork. Volunteering is rarely a solo mission; it's all about collaboration. You learn to navigate different personalities, align your efforts towards a common goal, and support your teammates. It's like being part of a band—each member plays a different instrument, but you all need to be in sync to create harmony. These aren't just handy skills for your resume; they're real-world abilities that boost your confidence and competence in any group setting.

Finding the right volunteer opportunity is like choosing the perfect app for your phone—it needs to fit your interests and schedule. Start by considering what causes you're passionate about. Is it animal welfare, environmental conservation, or perhaps community welfare? Once you've pinpointed your interest, look for organizations that work in these areas. Check out local non-profits, community centers, and even online platforms that list volunteering opportunities. Schools often have groups or clubs that require volunteer hours or check community service boards or clubs that can connect you with ongoing projects. The key is to choose something that resonates with you because when you're passionate about the cause, the work feels more like a hobby and less like a chore.

Volunteering also offers a unique avenue for personal growth. It's one thing to boost your social skills and pad up your college applications, but the real win is how it makes you feel about yourself. Each task completed, each thank-you received, adds a brick to your self-esteem. You're not just making a difference in the community; you're proving to yourself that you can impact the world, one volunteer hour at a time. This sense of accomplishment is a powerful boost to your self-worth, reminding you that you have valuable skills and a big heart.

So, as you step into the world of volunteering, think of it as more than just giving your time. It's about growing, learning, and connecting in ways that classrooms and textbooks can't match. It's about crafting a version of yourself that's not just more skilled but more open, empathetic, and ready to take on whatever challenges come your way. Whether you're planting trees, tutoring kids, or helping at a senior center, each experience is a step toward becoming a more engaged, empathetic, and skilled member of your community. So go ahead, find your cause, and dive in. The gains are bound to be more than just social; they're transformative.

Learning from Social Failures: A Growth Mindset

Exploring the social landscape can often resemble attempting to master an unfamiliar video game on its toughest difficulty setting — without a guide to the controls. It's natural to stumble and face setbacks along the way. But here's the scoop—every misstep is not a step back, but a step up to your next big leap. Think of social setbacks as those intense workout sessions. Sure, they leave you a bit sore, but they're also building your strength, resilience, and skills. Understanding that these bumps in the road are not just inevitable but invaluable can transform your approach from dread to readiness.

When you hit a social snag, whether it's an awkward conversation that went south or a joke that landed like a lead balloon, the natural reaction might be to replay it over and over in your head. Instead, flip the script. Start seeing these moments as golden opportunities for analysis and growth. Break down the interaction: What went well? What fizzled? Was there a moment where the tide turned? This isn't about beating yourself up—it's about becoming a social detective, uncovering clues that lead to better outcomes next time. For instance, if you realized that your joke didn't land because it was a bit too niche, next time you might choose something more relatable.

Turning our attention to those instances that leave us cringing, we recognize these as part of the human experience. It's exactly these uncomfortable situations that act as powerful motivators for personal growth. Reflecting on what prompts this discomfort—whether it's apprehension about others' opinions or not knowing the right words to say—provides significant insights into our development journey. By pinpointing these triggers, we can devise targeted strategies for improvement, transforming moments of awkwardness into invaluable lessons for our social toolkit. Whether it's enhancing your collection of conversation starters or boosting your confidence through public speaking, each awkward moment is an opportunity to learn more about yourself and take a step forward in your personal growth journey. Encountering situations that leave us wishing for an escape hatch is a universal experience. Yet, it's precisely these moments of discomfort that serve as catalysts for growth. Reflecting on what triggers this unease—be it the fear of judgment or the uncertainty of how to engage in conversation—can significantly inform our personal development strategy. Whether it's bolstering your arsenal of conversation openers or enhancing your public speaking prowess, each episode of discomfort is a stepping stone towards greater self-awareness and confidence. Identifying these triggers allows for targeted self-improvement, turning awkward moments into valuable lessons for future encounters. Ever had those moments where you wished the floor would swallow you up? Yep, we've all been there. But discomfort has its perks. It pushes you out of your comfort zone, and this is where real growth happens. Reflect on what made you uncomfortable. Was it the fear of being judged? The anxiety of not knowing what to say? Identifying these triggers can help you prepare better. Maybe you need to arm yourself with a few more conversation starters, or perhaps it's about building up your confidence with more public speaking. Each uncomfortable situation teaches you a bit more about yourself and nudges you toward personal development.

Handling setbacks constructively is the real game-changer. Next time you find yourself in a less-than-stellar social situation, take a strategic pause. Instead of spiraling into self-doubt, ask yourself, "What can I learn from this?" Maybe you need to work on your timing, or perhaps it's about reading the room better. Set small, achievable goals for your next interaction. It could be something as simple as making eye contact or ensuring your body language is open and inviting. These actionable steps are your building blocks to a more confident and competent social persona.

Developing a growth mindset is the ultimate goal here. This means seeing every social interaction, good or bad, as a chance to learn and improve. Embrace the idea that your social skills are a work in progress, and like any skill, they get better the more you practice. With a growth mindset, you're not chained to your past mistakes—they're just stepping stones to your next success. This mindset encourages resilience, a crucial ingredient for navigating the social world with grace and confidence. It allows you to bounce back from setbacks faster and keeps you motivated to keep pushing your boundaries.

By understanding the value of social failures, analyzing your interactions, learning from discomfort, and embracing constructive strategies for handling setbacks, you're setting yourself up for a rich, dynamic social life. Each step forward, no matter how small, is a piece of the puzzle in mastering the art of human connections. So, keep your head up, your mind open, and your spirit ready to learn. The social path is a winding one, filled with learning opportunities at every bend, and you have what it takes to walk it bravely.

Remember, the journey through social landscapes is rich with lessons and opportunities for growth. Embracing each experience, whether a triumph or a stumble, shapes you into a more adept social navigator. With a growth mindset, every interaction is a chance to expand your understanding and enhance your skills, propelling you towards becoming a more confident and resilient individual.

Dating: Building Healthy and Respectful Relationships

S tepping into the world of dating is a bit like learning to drive. It's exciting, a bit nerve-wracking, and loaded with new rules to follow. But instead of traffic signs, you're navigating emotions, and instead of road maps, you're figuring out how to communicate your feelings. Dating can feel like trying to assemble IKEA furniture without the instructions—confusing at times, but immensely rewarding when done right. This chapter is your missing manual, aimed to guide you through the complexities of dating relationships with ease, humor, and a healthy dose of reality checks.

Communicating and Understanding Boundaries

In the great game of dating, clarity is your best friend. Think about the last time you tried to guess someone's feelings based on their emojis alone. Confusing, right? Now, apply that to dating—it's crucial to say what you mean and mean what you say. Clear communication starts with being honest with yourself about what you feel and what you want out of a relationship. Are you looking for a casual hangout buddy, or are you aiming for a heart-and-flowers romance? Knowing this helps you communicate your intentions clearly, avoiding the "I thought we were just friends!" kind of drama.

Let's say you've got a crush. Instead of dropping subtle hints or hoping they'll read your mind (spoiler: they won't), why not express your interest directly? It could be something as simple as, "Hey, I've really enjoyed getting to know you and would love to hang out more. Maybe more than friends?" Yes, it takes guts, but it also cuts through the ambiguity that often makes dating feel like a bad mystery novel.

Clear communication also involves being honest about your feelings. If you're happy, say it! If something bothers you, speak up! It's like being in the driver's seat; if you don't steer, how can you expect to get where you want to go? Remember, being open about your feelings isn't just about making speeches; it's about having conversations. Listen to their responses, engage with their feelings, and build a dialogue. This back-and-forth communication is what helps relationships grow stronger and healthier.

Boundaries in dating are like personal rules that help you feel safe and respected—they define what's okay and what's not okay for you. These can range from how much time you spend together, to physical boundaries, to how you're comfortable communicating. Setting boundaries isn't about building walls; it's about laying out your personal comfort map for others to understand.

Start by knowing your limits. What makes you feel uncomfortable? How much space do you need? Communicating these boundaries clearly to your partner is key. It can be as straightforward as saying, "I need some alone time to recharge after school, so I might not text back right away. It's not that I don't want to talk, but I need some space to unwind." This kind of honesty helps prevent misunderstandings and shows that you respect yourself and your needs, which is super attractive, by the way!

Respecting boundaries also means being attentive to how comfortable your partner is. If you sense hesitation or discomfort, it's important to pull back and discuss it. Never pressure someone to move past their comfort zone, especially in physical aspects of a relationship. Respecting each other's boundaries builds trust and deepens your connection. After all, a good relationship is like a team—it only works when both players are on the same page.

Consent is a critical, non-negotiable part of any relationship, especially when it comes to dating. It's about having a clear and enthusiastic agreement before moving forward with any level of physical intimacy. Consent should always be freely given, reversible, informed, enthusiastic, and specific. Remember, consent can't be presumed from past actions; it must be clearly and actively given every time.

Educating yourself and your partner about consent is crucial. It's more than just the absence of a no; it's the presence of a yes. You can start the conversation with something like, "I want to make sure we're both totally comfortable, so let's check in with each other before things go further. Is this okay?" This creates a safe environment for both of you to express your feelings and desires openly.

Understanding consent clearly is pivotal in the dating scene. It safeguards you and your partner, laying the groundwork for a relationship rooted in respect and kindness. This clear grasp ensures your connection flourishes without misunderstandings or unease.

Venturing into the dating world may initially appear intimidating, yet armed with the proper mindset and strategies, it transforms into an enriching adventure of discovery—both of others and of your own self. By mastering the art of clear communication, respecting personal boundaries, and understanding the importance of consent, you're well on your way to building healthy and fulfilling relationships. So buckle up, be yourself, and enjoy the ride into the world of dating, where every experience—whether a brief encounter or a long-term romance—offers a chance to learn, grow, and connect.

Digital Interaction: Communication and Social Media

I f navigating the digital world was a video game, texting would undoubtedly be one of those tricky levels where the rewards are super high, but so are the risks of epic fails. Welcome to the realm of digital communication, where a simple text can either make your day or turn into a puzzling riddle of emojis and slang. Think of this chapter as your cheat sheet to mastering this level with flair, ensuring every DM or text enhances your social life instead of complicating it.

Texting Etiquette: Clear and Effective Communication

Let's kick things off with a core principle: clarity in texting is like the GPS for your conversations. It helps your message reach its destination without unnecessary detours. Ever received a text so long and winding that you need to sit down with a cup of tea and a detective hat just to decipher it? Yeah, not fun. Brevity is your best buddy when it comes to texting. It's about getting to the point without building a labyrinth around it. But, and this is a big but, there are times when a longer, detailed text is necessary—like explaining why you can't make it to a friend's party or discussing plans that involve several steps. The trick is to know when a quick text suffices and when something warrants a more in-depth conversation, possibly even a call or face-to-face chat. Remember, if your message takes more than a minute to type out, perhaps texting isn't the right tool for the job.

Emojis and slang are the spices of text conversations—they can add flavor, but definitely can overpower the dish if not used wisely. Emojis are great for conveying emotions or adding a playful tone, making sure your friend knows that your "I'm going to kill you" is a joke because you paired it with a laughing emoji. However, splattering emojis like confetti in every message might confuse or distract from the main message. Likewise, slang keeps your texts casual and relatable but imagine receiving a text that's more abbreviations than words. Use slang and emojis thoughtfully, ensuring they enrich the message, not encrypt it.

Texting's Achilles' heel? Tone. Without facial expressions or voice inflections, even a simple "Okay" can be a minefield. Is it an "Okay, I'm excited!" or an "Okay, I'm disappointed"? To avoid misunderstandings, it's crucial to be mindful of how your words might come across. When in doubt, add a little more context or tweak your word choice. Instead of a curt "Fine," maybe say "Sure, that sounds good!" if you're genuinely okay with the plans. It's about painting a clear emotional backdrop so that your true feelings shine through the digital curtain.

It's easy for text conversations to spiral out of control. Acting on impulse, like snapping back with a sharp retort when you're offended, comes naturally; however, crafting a thoughtful response is more of an acquired skill. This means sometimes you need to hit the pause button—put your phone aside for a second—and think about a reply that's both thoughtful and positive. This approach is crucial during tense conversations. Rash reactions can turn small disagreements into big arguments, while measured replies can calm stormy waters. Practice patience in your texts, particularly when emotions run high or the conversation is important. Think of it as hitting a pause button in an intense video game, buying you time to consider your next action carefully.

Have you ever hit "send" on a text message only to immediately wish you could snatch it back from the digital ether? Autocorrect mishaps and typos can awkwardly transform "I'm busy" into "I'm busty," turning a straightforward conversation into an embarrassing mix-up. Taking a moment to review your message before sending it can prevent many red-faced apologies and clarifications later. This brief pause is a small investment that pays off by ensuring your messages are both clear and free of mortifying mistakes. While texting doesn't require the same immediate back-and-forth as talking in person, the timing of your responses can still significantly impact your conversations. Prompt replies convey your interest and respect for the person on the other end of the conversation. But being prompt doesn't mean you need to be constantly available. Striking the right balance means responding in a timely manner without compromising your own time and commitments. If you're tied up with another task, a simple "Can I get back to you in an hour?" not only manages expectations but also demonstrates that you value your time and theirs.

Avoiding texting pitfalls—such as using ALL CAPS (which can come across as shouting), overdoing it with abbreviations (your texts shouldn't need deciphering), or sending messages late at night (manners matter 24/7)—helps prevent misinterpretation and maintains digital decorum. By side-stepping these common errors, your messages will be understood exactly as you intend, free from unintended offense or confusion. When it comes to sexting, tread carefully. This area not only tests your judgment but also your ethical stance and legal knowledge. The consequences can vary widely, from embarrassment to facing serious legal issues, particularly for minors. Prioritize safety: resist any pressure to send explicit content and always honor personal boundaries. Should you ever be on the receiving end of unsolicited inappropriate content, remember it's not your fault, and reach out to a trusted adult for support. In professional contexts, such as texting a boss or teacher, aim for clarity and formality. Skip the casual abbreviations and emojis. Begin with a polite greeting, communicate your message succinctly, and close with a respectful farewell. This approach demonstrates your respect and professionalism, ensuring your texts accurately convey your commitment to your responsibilities or education. Mastering the art of digital communication might sometimes feel as challenging as decoding ancient scripts, but armed with these strategies, you'll be equipped to navigate text conversations with ease.

From casual chats with friends to more sensitive discussions or professional exchanges, these guidelines will help you maintain smooth and effective digital interactions.

Creating Impactful Online Profiles

Creating an online profile isn't just about uploading a couple of selfies and your favorite quote; it's like giving a digital handshake. This is your introduction to the world, whether on social media or professional platforms like LinkedIn. The goal is to create a cohesive and positive online presence that authentically represents you. It's about telling your story in a way that resonates with your audience, from future employers to new friends worldwide.

Imagine visiting someone's social media page and instantly getting a sense of who they are and what they're about. That's the power of a well-crafted profile. Begin by selecting a profile picture that is clear, approachable, and a true reflection of yourself. Remember, this image often serves as your first introduction, so ensure it leaves a positive and memorable impression. Next, your bio should act as your elevator pitch. Who are you? What are your passions? What makes you unique? Keep it concise but expressive, showcasing your personality, whether it's humor, artistic flair, or a love for coding.

Highlight your achievements, share your interests, and post about your experiences. Whether it's a new painting, a challenging math test you aced, or a recent adventure, these snippets make your profile stand out and tell a more complete story of who you are. Each post contributes to the overall image you're projecting, so ensure it aligns with the persona you want to present.

Follow public figures or influencers who reflect the values and image you aspire to. Observe how they communicate, the content they share, and their engagement style. These observations can provide valuable lessons in personal branding and interaction. However, always adapt these inspirations to fit your authentic self. Learn from the best, then make it your own.

Consistency is crucial. Whether someone finds you on Instagram, TikTok, or LinkedIn, they should recognize it's the same person behind the screen. This doesn't mean all your posts need to look the same, but maintaining a consistent tone and quality helps strengthen your personal brand and build trust. If you're playful and geeky on TikTok, let some of that charm shine through on your other profiles as well.

Crafting your online profile is like painting a self-portrait. Each choice, from the emojis to the tone, shapes how the world sees you. By focusing on a cohesive, positive, and authentic presentation, you ensure that this digital portrait is striking and true to who you are. Take control of your online identity and mold it with intention and care, making every pixel count in the digital landscape.

Social Media: Positive Engagement and Online Etiquette

Navigating social media might feel like trying to be heard in a loud, crowded room. Yet, within this complexity, there's a chance to create a meaningful online identity. Your social media accounts are like personal billboards. What you post, share, and comment on crafts your digital reputation, opening doors to friendships, career opportunities, and even college prospects. Here's how to harness this tool to build a reputation you can be proud of.

Envision walking into an interview and discovering the interviewer is already impressed by your online presence. They've checked out your accomplishments on LinkedIn and your active involvement in community projects shared on Facebook, identifying you as an exceptional applicant. This highlights the importance of cultivating a positive online identity—it's a powerful advocate for your talents, character, and goals, opening doors to opportunities in both your career and personal life. It goes beyond mere popularity or viral moments; it's about consistently projecting an image that mirrors your genuine values, interests, and professional demeanor.

Ensure your social media activity paints you in the best light by starting with positivity. In a world where online interactions can quickly turn negative, being a beacon of positivity sets you apart. Share uplifting and inspiring content, celebrate others' achievements, and spread good vibes. When commenting, keep it constructive and supportive. Your words can uplift others or bring them down, so choose to be the reason someone smiles when they check their notifications.

Leverage your social platforms to spotlight issues close to your heart, disseminate valuable insights, and rally support.

Whether you're boosting a community initiative on Instagram or supporting a local nonprofit through tweets, your social presence can catalyze tangible change. This approach not only showcases your leadership and compassion but also underscores your proactive spirit.

Consistency in communication is also key. If you're passionate about mental health, let your posts reflect that regularly. A consistent theme or voice helps people understand who you are and what you stand for, creating a stronger connection with your audience. Let your true self shine through, whether through inspirational quotes, advocacy posts, or personal stories.

In our digitally-driven world, being clear and coherent in your communication is crucial. Crafting messages that are easy to understand and relate to can significantly enhance your digital footprint. For more formal or diverse audiences, steer clear of shorthand or slang. Opt for complete sentences, correct punctuation, and a tone that's appropriate for the situation. When in doubt about posting something, apply the "grandma rule": if it's not something you'd want your grandmother to see, it's probably best not to share it.

Approaching the world of social media with a positive outlook, clear intent, and a purposeful attitude can transform your online interactions, laying the groundwork for a digital identity that truly represents who you are. Every action you take online—every like, share, and comment—contributes to a digital footprint that can open new opportunities and forge valuable connections. Therefore, whenever you're about to update your status or post a new comment, pause and consider the impact of your words and actions.

Let them be a force for good, reflecting your best self and making a meaningful difference.

Handling Cyberbullying

Imagine you're chilling in your digital playground, scrolling through your favorite social platforms, when suddenly, you stumble across a comment or message that feels like a virtual punch in the gut. Welcome to the not-so-fun side of the internet—cyberbullying. It's like the school bully found a way into your safe space, your personal escape room—the digital world. Cyberbullying includes any form of bullying that happens online or through smartphones and tablets. This could be mean texts, rumors sent through email, or embarrassing photos posted on social media.

Cyberbullying can take many forms, and it's important to recognize them so you can take action. Common examples include nasty comments, which are hurtful or derogatory remarks on your posts, photos, or videos. Hurtful messages directly insult, threaten, or demean you through private messaging. Humiliating photos or videos involve sharing images or videos without your consent to embarrass or shame you. Spreading rumors entails sharing false or malicious information to damage your reputation. Making fun in group chats is a subtle form of bullying where you're singled out or mocked in group conversations. Exclusion involves deliberately leaving someone out of online groups or activities, making them feel isolated. Impersonation is creating fake profiles or accounts to impersonate you and post harmful content. Doxxing involves sharing personal information like your address or phone number without your permission. Cyberstalking includes repeatedly sending threatening or intimidating messages, often causing fear for your safety. Finally, harassment is persistent and aggressive behavior aimed at intimidating or upsetting you.

The impact of cyberbullying can be profound and long-lasting. Victims often experience feelings of anxiety, depression, and isolation, which can affect their mental health and overall well-being. The pervasive nature of digital technology means that cyberbullying can occur at any time, making it difficult for victims to find relief. Unlike traditional bullying, which might end when the school day does, cyberbullying can follow you home, invading your personal space and making you feel as though there's no escape. The emotional distress caused by cyberbullying can lead to decreased academic performance, withdrawal from social activities, and even physical symptoms like headaches or stomach aches. In severe cases, the stress and humiliation can contribute to self-harm or suicidal thoughts. The permanence of online posts also means that the damage can be enduring; humiliating content can be shared widely and remain accessible for years, making the victim feel continuously exposed and vulnerable.

If you find yourself a target of cyberbullying, remember you have the power to take action. Start by blocking or unfollowing the bully to cut off their access to your online presence. Most social media platforms have features that allow you to report abusive behavior; don't hesitate to use them. Reporting the behavior not only helps protect you but also alerts the platform to potentially harmful users. Saving evidence of the bullying is crucial. Take screenshots of mean comments, hurtful messages, or any other forms of abuse.

This documentation can be essential if you need to report the behavior to authorities, school officials, or even the platform itself. Having a record of the incidents can help build a case and ensure that appropriate action is taken against the bully.

Stand up for friends who are being bullied and encourage others to do the same. When you see someone being targeted, offer them support by speaking out against the bullying and showing them they're not alone. Sometimes, just letting someone know you care can make a huge difference. Reach out to friends who seem down or withdrawn and offer your support. Encouraging open communication about cyberbullying can also help others feel more comfortable seeking help if they become targets.

Promote positive interactions by being a role model for kindness and respect online. Share uplifting content, celebrate others' achievements, and encourage constructive dialogue. By fostering a positive online environment, you can help reduce the incidence of cyberbullying and create a safer space for everyone.

Education is key to preventing cyberbullying. Learn about the different forms it can take and how to handle them. Understanding the signs of cyberbullying and knowing what actions to take can empower you and others to respond effectively. Share this knowledge with your peers through discussions, presentations, or social media posts. Raise awareness about the impact of cyberbullying and the importance of creating a supportive online community. Schools and communities can also play a role by providing resources and support for those affected. Workshops, counseling services, and anti-bullying campaigns can help educate and protect students. Encouraging schools to incorporate digital citizenship into their curriculum can help students learn about responsible online behavior and the consequences of cyberbullying. By fostering an environment of respect and empathy, we can work towards reducing the prevalence of cyberbullying and supporting those who are affected.

Exploring the digital world is fraught with obstacles, yet through awareness, proactive measures, and mutual support, we can transform the internet into a welcoming and secure environment for all. Keep in mind, your online realm ought to be a sanctuary where you're respected, cherished, and empowered to express your true self.

Balancing Online and Offline Friendships

In a world where a 'like' can feel like a warm hug from across cyberspace, it's crucial to remember the irreplaceable value of face-to-face interactions. Think about it: when was the last time an emoji gave you a high-five or a meme sat down for a coffee chat? Exactly. Real-life interactions pack a punch that digital communication just can't match. They allow us to connect on a deeper level, picking up on subtle nuances like tone of voice, facial expressions, and body language, all of which are lost in the digital realm. These in-person connections foster stronger bonds and a deeper understanding of each other, something that's hard to achieve through a screen.

However, balancing our online and offline worlds is kind of like trying to stand on a seesaw. Lean too much on one side, and you might find yourself missing out on the benefits of the other. It's about finding that sweet spot where both can coexist without overshadowing each other. Setting boundaries with digital communication is key. It's tempting to be constantly connected, but too much screen time can lead to a sort of friendship fatigue, where your real-life interactions start to suffer because you're just too zapped from your digital ones. Try designating certain times of the day or specific days of the week as digital detox times, where you consciously unplug and give your full attention to the people physically around you. This not only helps in keeping your real-world relationships healthy but also gives you a much-needed break from the digital chatter.

Digital tools, when used thoughtfully, can actually enhance your personal relationships rather than detract from them. Think of how a simple calendar app can help you manage get-togethers, or how a quick text can remind a friend about an upcoming event. These tools become extensions of your intent to stay connected, acting as bridges between your digital and physical worlds. For instance, sharing a funny video with a friend can be a great way to brighten their day and show that you're thinking of them, building a connection that can be deepened when you next meet in person. It's about using these tools to complement, not replace, the face-to-face interactions that form the bedrock of deep, enduring friendships.

By mixing your online and offline hangouts, you're building a great network of friendships that's both wide and deep. It's all about getting the best of both worlds—using the convenience and reach of digital tools while still enjoying the unbeatable vibes of in-person connections. You're not picking one over the other; instead, you're letting them boost each other, creating a fuller, more connected life.

Privacy and Safety in Digital Communication

Think of your digital footprint like a permanent marker; everything you share, post, or react to online can stick around much longer than you might expect. This can be awesome when you're showing off cool vacation pics, but not so much when it comes to impulsive rants or unflattering photos from a party. It's important to think about how your digital footprint could be viewed by future employers, college admissions boards, or even future romantic partners. Every post, comment, and like can either open doors for you or close them. So, ask yourself: what story do you want your online persona to tell?

Adjusting privacy settings on social media is like customizing the settings in a video game. You get to decide which parts of your life are visible to everyone and which parts stay private. Platforms like Facebook, Instagram, and Twitter have plenty of privacy tools to help you control who sees your posts, who can tag you, and who can comment. Take the time to explore these settings and tailor them to what makes you feel comfortable. Maybe you want everyone to see your art projects to gain more followers, but you prefer only close friends to see your birthday photos. Understanding and using these settings helps you take control of your online story.

Let's get a bit techy—data privacy. Ever notice ads for things you've just talked about? That's because of data collection. Your online actions, like the videos you watch or the searches you make, can be tracked, analyzed, and sold. Reading the terms of service and privacy policies of the platforms you use is like reading the rules of a game. It might be boring, but it's important. Knowing what data you're sharing and how it's used helps you make smart choices about where and how you engage online. Oversharing on the internet is like giving out too many copies of your house key; it can lead to trouble. Sharing too much can make you vulnerable to risks like identity theft or cyberbullying. It might be tempting to share every detail of your life, but remember, the internet is not your personal diary. Be careful about what you post. Sharing about a family trip is usually okay, but announcing that your house is empty can be risky. The less personal info you put out there, the safer you are.

Staying secure online is super important. Use strong, unique passwords, enable two-factor authentication, and watch out for phishing attempts—those are fake messages trying to steal your personal info. Keep your software updated and be cautious about the links you click or files you download. Protect your devices like you would your personal space—keep them locked and secure. When browsing online, think of it like wearing a seatbelt. Stick to trustworthy sites, especially when shopping or downloading content. Those offers for free iPhones on sketchy websites? Probably scams. And those fun quizzes that promise to tell you your personality based on random questions? They often collect your data. Navigating the online world safely isn't just about avoiding risks; it's about enjoying the positives wisely and carefully.

By managing your digital footprint, fine-tuning your privacy settings, making smart choices about what you share, and following safe online practices, you create a safer, more positive digital life. This approach protects you and ensures that your online presence shows off the best version of you, now and in the future. Remember, the online world is an extension of the real world. The connections you make, the information you share, and the footprints you leave all shape how you grow, learn, and interact in the digital age.

Your Journey Forward

Our journey has been about empowering introverted and socially anxious teens to thrive in social situations by overcoming fears and building practical social skills. You are now equipped with the tools and insights needed to navigate the social world with confidence and grace. As you stand on the threshold of your future, it's time to take what you've learned and step boldly into the next phase of your life. Remember, you have the ability to transform your interactions and relationships.

One of the most valuable lessons you can carry forward is the power of authenticity. In a world that often pressures you to conform, staying true to yourself is a profound strength. Authenticity means embracing your unique qualities, values, and perspectives. It's about being honest in your interactions and expressing your true self. When you are authentic, you attract genuine connections and build trust with others. Remember, it's not about fitting in, but about standing out and being appreciated for who you truly are.

Life is filled with challenges and setbacks, and building resilience is key to navigating these obstacles. Resilience is the ability to bounce back from difficulties and continue moving forward. Develop a mindset that views challenges as opportunities for growth. Practice self-compassion and remind yourself that it's okay to make mistakes. Each setback is a learning experience that brings you closer to becoming a stronger, more capable individual. By fostering resilience, you'll find that you can handle social situations with greater ease and confidence.

Empathy is at the heart of meaningful relationships. It involves understanding and sharing the feelings of others. Cultivate empathy by actively listening to those around you, putting yourself in their shoes, and showing genuine concern for their well-being. Empathy helps you connect on a deeper level, resolve conflicts more effectively, and create a supportive environment. Remember, everyone has their own struggles and stories, and a little empathy can go a long way in building lasting bonds.

Effective communication is a cornerstone of social success. It's not just about what you say, but how you say it. Pay attention to non-verbal cues, such as body language and facial expressions, and ensure your words align with your actions. Practice active listening, where you fully engage with the speaker and respond thoughtfully. Clear and respectful communication helps prevent misunderstandings and builds stronger, more trusting relationships. Whether you're speaking to a friend, family member, or stranger, strive to communicate with clarity and kindness.

Setting boundaries is essential for maintaining healthy relationships and personal well-being. Boundaries define what is acceptable and what is not, and they help protect your emotional and mental health. Learn to say no when necessary and communicate your limits clearly and respectfully. Respecting others' boundaries is equally important. By setting and respecting boundaries, you create a balanced and respectful social environment where everyone feels safe and valued.

Your social journey is unique to you. Set realistic and achievable social goals, celebrate your progress and be patient with yourself as you continue to grow. Don't be too hard on yourself for mistakes; every misstep is an opportunity to learn and improve. Maintain a positive attitude and believe in your ability to grow and thrive socially. Use your new skills to help your friends and make your social circle even better. Share what you've learned and create a positive vibe by lending a hand when someone needs it. Support those who find social situations tricky; your encouragement can make a big difference.

Keep pushing yourself to learn and grow by seeking out workshops, seminars, books, and articles on social skills, leadership, and personal growth. Always be open to discovering new things about yourself and others. Watch YouTube tutorials, follow social media influencers who share tips, or join online communities that discuss social skills. Each new thing you learn can boost your confidence and enhance your social abilities. You've already equipped yourself with valuable tools and strategies to overcome social anxiety, communicate effectively, and build strong relationships. Step out of your comfort zone, empower yourself, and thrive socially.

Your future is filled with potential, and you have the power to shape your social world and create a fulfilling, connected life. Remember, the journey is just as important as the destination. Celebrate your successes, learn from your failures, and always strive to be the best version of yourself.

You are not alone in your struggle with social anxiety or awkwardness. With dedication and practice, you can overcome any social challenge. May your path forward be filled with growth, connection, and fulfillment. Here's to your continued growth and success!

Unlocking Social Skills for Teens

Now that you have everything you need to thrive socially, it's time to share what you've learned and help others find the same support.

Hey there, amazing reader!

You've made it to the end of "Unlocking Social Skills for Teens" by Kimberly Myrick—way to go! With all the skills and strategies you've picked up, you're ready to take on any social situation with confidence. But before you go, there's one more thing you can do to make a difference.

By leaving a review on Amazon, you can guide other teens to this book, helping them find the support they need to overcome social anxiety and build their own social skills. Your honest opinion could be exactly what someone else needs to see.

Thank you for being part of this journey. Social skills grow stronger when we share what we've learned, and your review helps keep that knowledge alive.

Thank you for spreading the word and helping others find their way. Keep using your social skills to connect, grow, and make the world a friendlier place!

- Your biggest fan, Kimberly Myrick

Resources

Books

"How to Win Friends and Influence People" by Dale Carnegie
A classic book on effective communication and building relationships.

"The 7 Habits of Highly Effective Teens" by Sean Covey
A guide to personal development and building healthy habits.

"Emotional Intelligence 2.0" by Travis Bradberry and Jean Greaves
A practical book on understanding and improving emotional intelligence.

"Quiet: The Power of Introverts in a World That Can't Stop Talking" by Susan Cain
Insightful read on the strengths of introverts and how they can thrive socially.

"The Social Skills Guidebook" by Chris MacLeod
A comprehensive guide on improving social skills and building confidence.

Websites

TeensHealth
Offers articles and advice on mental health, communication, and relationships.

The Social Skills Guidebook
Provides practical tips and strategies for improving social skills.
MindTools
Offers tools and resources for leadership, communication, and personal development.

Apps

Headspace
A mindfulness app that helps improve focus, reduce stress, and enhance emotional well-being.
Happify
Uses games and activities to improve emotional health and resilience.
7 Cups
Provides emotional support and counseling through chats with trained listeners.

References

- *31 Icebreaker Games For Teens For ANY Situation* https://www. scienceofpeople.com/icebreakers-for-teens/
- *Understanding Body Language In Social Settings* https://www. betterhelp.com/advice/body-language/understanding-body-language-in-social-settings/
- *50 Conversation Starters to Build Communication with Teens* https:// www.signupgenius.com/home/teen-conversation-topics.cfm
- *How to Practice Active Listening: 16 Examples & Techniques* https:// positivepsychology.com/active-listening-techniques/
- *7 deep breathing exercises to help you calm anxiety* https://www.calm. com/blog/breathing-exercises-for-anxiety#:~
- *How to Teach Social Skills Through Role-Playing* https://blog.esc13. net/how-to-teach-social-skills-through-role-playing/
- *The Effect of Visualization Techniques on Students ...* https://www. ncbi.nlm.nih.gov/pmc/articles/PMC9691158/
- *Differences Between Shyness and Social Anxiety Disorder* https:// www.verywellmind.com/difference-between-shyness-and-social-anxiety-disorder-3024431
- *How to Ask Open-Ended Questions: 20 Examples* https://www. mentimeter.com/blog/stand-out-get-ahead/how-to-create-open-ended-questions
- *11 Tips for Talking to Someone You Disagree With* https://www. psychologytoday.com/us/blog/brave-talk/202101/11-tips-talking-someone-you-disagree
- *Brand Storytelling Made Easy with These 5 Story Elements* https:// bairstories.com/the-5-story-elements-needed-for-storytelling
- *Cultural Differences in Humor Perception, Usage, and ...* https://www. frontiersin.org/journals/psychology/articles/10.3389/fpsyg. 2019.00123/full
- *Teens, Social Media and Technology 2023* https://www.pewresearch. org/internet/2023/12/11/teens-social-media-and-technology-2023/

- *Understanding Effective Online Communication - Mentoring.org* https://www.mentoring.org/wp-content/uploads/2022/01/BBM-Chapter-5.pdf
- *Teens digital footprints haunt their future opportunities* https://pantherprowler.org/teens-digital-footprints-haunt-their-future-opportunities/
- *A Guide to Conflict Resolution for Teens* https://mentalhealthcenterkids.com/blogs/articles/conflict-resolution-for-teens
- *Effective Strategies for Teaching Assertiveness in High School* https://everydayspeech.com/blog-posts/general/empowering-teens-effective-strategies-for-teaching-assertiveness-in-high-school/
- *Social Media's Effect on Self-Esteem: How Does It Affect ...* https://socialmediavictims.org/mental-health/self-esteem/
- *20 Ways to Avoid Peer Pressure* https://yourlifecounts.org/learning-center/peer-pressure/20-ways-to-avoid-peer-pressure/
- *8 Activities To Boost Teen Self-Esteem* https://www.embarkbh.com/blog/mental-health/self-esteem-activities-for-teens/
- *Teenagers and communication* https://www.betterhealth.vic.gov.au/health/healthyliving/teenagers-and-communication
- *Conflict Resolution Strategies - 7 Steps To Resolve Teen ...* https://paradigmtreatment.com/resolve-a-conflict-7-simple-steps/
- *10 Signs of a Toxic Friend (and How to Break Up With Them)* https://www.verywellmind.com/signs-of-a-toxic-friend-8430982
- *Building Strong Family Relationships | Cooperative Extension* https://www.udel.edu/canr/cooperative-extension/fact-sheets/building-strong-family-relationships/
- *Conflict Resolution Strategies - 7 Steps To Resolve Teen ...* https://paradigmtreatment.com/resolve-a-conflict-7-simple-steps/
- *18 Job Interview Tips for Teens they Need to Know* https://truenorthhomeschool.academy/18-job-interview-tips-for-teens-they-need-to-know/
- *Extracurricular Activities: Benefits and Balance* https://parentandteen.com/extracurricular-benefits-balance/
- *11 Public Speaking Tips for Youth (and Adults!) - VentureLab* https://venturelab.org/public-speaking-tips/
- *How to Help Teens Set Effective Goals (Tips & Templates)* https://biglifejournal.com/blogs/blog/guide-effective-goal-setting-teens-template-worksheet

- *The Power and Benefits of Mindfulness Meditation* https://childmind. org/article/the-power-of-mindfulness/
- *3 elements of successful youth advocacy work* https://truthinitiative. org/research-resources/tobacco-prevention-efforts/3-elements-successful-youth-advocacy-work
- *How a Growth Mindset Benefits Kids' Social-Emotional ...* https:// www.familius.com/growth-mindset-for-kids/